PRISONERS OF THE PURGE: THE VICTIMS OF TURKEY'S FAILING RULE OF LAW

HEARING

BEFORE THE

COMMISSION ON SECURITY AND COOPERATION IN EUROPE

ONE HUNDRED FIFTEENTH CONGRESS

FIRST SESSION

NOVEMBER 15, 2017

Printed for the use of the
Commission on Security and Cooperation in Europe

[CSCE 115–1–7]

Available via www.csce.gov

U.S. GOVERNMENT PUBLISHING OFFICE

27–643 PDF   WASHINGTON : 2018

For sale by the Superintendent of Documents, U.S. Government Publishing Office
Internet: bookstore.gpo.gov   Phone: toll free (866) 512–1800; DC area (202) 512–1800
Fax: (202) 512–2104   Mail: Stop IDCC, Washington, DC 20402–0001

PRISONERS OF THE PURGE: THE VICTIMS OF TURKEY'S FAILING RULE OF LAW

COMMISSIONERS

WITNESSES

APPENDIX

[III]

Page

MATERIAL FOR THE RECORD

PRISONERS OF THE PURGE: THE VICTIMS OF TURKEY'S FAILING RULE OF LAW

November 15, 2017

COMMISSION ON SECURITY AND COOPERATION IN EUROPE

WASHINGTON, DC

The hearing was held at 9:30 a.m. in Room 124, Dirksen Senate Office Building, Washington, DC, Hon. Thom Tillis, Commissioner, Commission on Security and Cooperation in Europe, presiding.

Commissioners present: Hon. Thom Tillis, Commissioner, Commission on Security and Cooperation in Europe; Hon. Michael C. Burgess, Commissioner, Commission on Security and Cooperation in Europe; Hon. Randy Hultgren, Commissioner, Commission on Security and Cooperation in Europe; Hon. Jeanne Shaheen, Commissioner, Commission on Security and Cooperation in Europe; Hon. Benjamin L. Cardin, Ranking Member, Commission on Security and Cooperation in Europe; and Hon. John Boozman, Commissioner, Commission on Security and Cooperation in Europe.

Witnesses present: Jonathan R. Cohen, Deputy Assistant Secretary, Bureau of European and Eurasian Affairs, U.S. Department of State; CeCe Heil, Executive Counsel, American Center for Law and Justice; Jacqueline Furnari, Daughter of Andrew Brunson; and Nate Schenkkan, Director of the Nations in Transit Project, Freedom House.

HON. THOM TILLIS, COMMISSIONER, COMMISSION ON SECURITY AND COOPERATION IN EUROPE

Mr. TILLIS. Good morning, everyone. This hearing of the Helsinki Commission will come to order.

I want to welcome everyone here to this Helsinki Commission hearing titled "Prisoners of the Purge: The Victims of Turkey's Failing Rule of Law." I'm honored to be chairing this hearing on behalf of Senator and Chairman Wicker.

As of today, an American pastor has spent 404 days in a Turkish jail without a trial, without access to evidence against him, the subject of a vicious smear campaign from the Turkish press, and facing life in prison on fabricated charges of being a terrorist and a coup plotter.

Elsewhere in Turkey, a Turkish-American NASA scientist has spent 480 days in prison, much of it in solitary confinement, on terrorism and espionage charges springing from a baseless testimony of a disgruntled relative and a bizarre compilation of circumstantial evidence, including a dollar bill seized from his parents' home.

(1)

Today also marks 253 days behind bars for a veteran Turkish employee of the U.S. consulate in Adana who stands accused of terrorism for doing his job as he has for 30 years: communicating on behalf of the United States Government with local community contacts.

These prisoners—Andrew Brunson, Serkan Gölge, and Hamza Uluçay—are the innocent victims of Turkey's collapsing rule of law. With every passing day, the injustice of these detentions compounds itself. For the Brunson family next week, another Thanksgiving apart. For Kubra and her two young kids, another day away from their home in Houston. For Hamza, another inexplicable punishment for his dedication to the job he loves.

But the focus of this hearing is not personal, it's principle. Just as Andrew, Serkan, and Hamza have been victims of Turkey's failing rule of law, there are literally thousands more like them behind bars today. Since imposing a state of emergency nearly 16 months ago, the Turkish Government has detained more than 60,000 people and fired or suspended upwards of 100,000 others from their jobs. The so-called Decree Laws authorizing these punitive measures do not establish any evidentiary standard for application, thereby permitting wide-scale abuse as seen in the cases I've highlighted.

Of course, context matters, and the Turkish Government invokes its constitutional state of emergency provisions in the wake of the July 2016 coup attempt, an unacceptable and violent attack on the constitutional order of a NATO ally—an attack I unequivocally condemn. But the question is not whether Turkey has the right to pursue justice after such a national trauma: the question is how it goes about it.

The Helsinki Commission has called this hearing today to get to the bottom of the accumulating injustices under the state of emergency. As a participating State of the Organization for Security and Cooperation in Europe, Turkey has committed itself to upholding certain rule-of-law standards even under extraordinary circumstances. Among these commitments is the guarantee of equality before the law.

However, Turkey's commitment to this principle has been called into serious question. Just two months ago, President Erdoğan proposed an outrageous swap: Andrew Brunson, a pastor, "for a pastor" in his words. If the United States would circumvent its rule of law to extradite a free man, Erdoğan suggested, then Turkey would release a wrongfully imprisoned one. Let us be clear about what President Erdoğan proposed: This is not justice; it's ransom. The United States should not expect, much less accept, this sort of treatment from a NATO ally.

The harassment and detention of our consulate staff has also overstepped the bounds of diplomatic conduct among partners. I was glad to see the State Department in the past month impose some real cost for this behavior by suspending non-immigrant visa services to Turkey. While the department announced last week that it had resumed these services on a limited basis and received assurances about the security of our local employees, I hope that we are clear with Turkey that we will not accept anything short of true and timely justice for our detained consulate staff and our citizens behind bars.

I also hope that we will not tire in advocating for the basic rights and freedoms of thousands of Turks impacted by these sweeping purges—academics, mayors, legislators, journalists, and human rights defenders among them.

Let me conclude by saying that it is in the interest of the United States to have Turkey as a strong and reliable ally. From strengthening NATO to fighting terrorism to resolving conflicts in the Middle East, we have important work to do together, and we will be more successful if we can work as partners. The urgency of these tasks underscores the importance of resolving distractions and rebuilding the trust we need to achieve common objectives. And, as always, our partners are strongest when they are rooted in shared principles.

We have two excellent panels of witnesses today to examine these topics, and I'll introduce the panels separately. But I would like to say at the outset that I am especially pleased to have with us a State Department witness, Deputy Assistant Secretary for European and Eurasian Affairs Jonathan Cohen, to provide the administration's perspective on these developments, U.S. policy towards Turkey, and the future of the bilateral relationship.

I'm also honored to have on our second panel Jacqueline Furnari, Andrew Brunson's daughter, from my State of North Carolina, and I understand a proud student of UNC Chapel Hill.

Before I introduce the panels, though, I'd like to offer my fellow commissioners an opportunity to make opening statements.

HON. MICHAEL C. BURGESS, COMMISSIONER, COMMISSION ON SECURITY AND COOPERATION IN EUROPE

Mr. BURGESS. Well, thank you, Senator Tillis. Thank you, Secretary, for agreeing to be here this morning. And I want to thank the Helsinki Commission for convening the hearing on what has been a pressing issue since July of 2016.

Five days ago, Turkish and American leaders gathered at the Republic's New York City consulate to commemorate the life and legacy of Mustafa Kemal Atatürk, one of modern history's great reformers. Following the conclusion of World War I, Atatürk sought to create a democracy based on the rule of law amidst the ashes of the Ottoman Empire.

As with all democracies, the Republic of Turkey has had its share of challenges and triumphs. Since its formation, Turkey has balanced between its constitutional secularism and its religious heritage. From the recognition of the Lausanne Treaty in 1923, there have been concerns that the country's religious population is under attack by its secularists. All the while, fear that Turkey will fall back into a country dominated by religious hardliners remains an inescapable concern. The constant battle between the two extremes I'm certain has left many Turks unsure of who or what will come next.

Most recently, the failed coup of July 2016—and I join with Senator Tillis in condemning in the strongest possible terms that activity—but that left the country clawing its self-inflicted wounds. Though carried out by military groups purportedly upholding

Atatürk's original vision for the country, it is hard to believe that the Republic's founder would have supported open insurrection and violence in the streets, clashes between military and civilians, or the imprisonment of innocents.

The uprising resulted in a widespread response by President Erdoğan and his ruling Justice and Development Party. Unfortunately, the crackdown has left nearly 50,000 people incarcerated. And within this massive group are a dozen American citizens, including Pastor Andrew Brunson and NASA scientist Serkan Gölge. These Americans, along with many of their Turkish counterparts, have only a tenuous charge against them: that they are agents and activists of Fethullah Gülen.

Mr. Gülen—a Muslim leader in teaching a tolerant, outward approach to Islam—is yet another individual who the Turkish Government has decided to indict with almost no evidence. Despite an alliance between the Justice and Development Party and the Gülenists at the onset of Mr. Erdoğan's political ascendancy, the two leaders suffered a breakdown in relations. Following the failed coup, the Erdoğan government leveled charges against the cleric, claiming that he planned and incited the attempted regime change. Mr. Gülen has been living in self-imposed exile in Pennsylvania since 1999.

Though the Turkish Government submitted a formal request for the extradition of Mr. Gülen, neither the State Department nor the Justice Department has received any information that would cause the United States to comply with this request. The Turkish Government has repeated, and with no evidence made the claim that Mr. Gülen funds schools, including some public schools in my home State of Texas, to radicalize students against the current Turkish Government.

Though I am opposed to much of what President Erdoğan does, I respect Turkish sovereignty and their self-determination. However, when the president begins targeting American citizens, especially our children, this is a bridge too far.

In another incident early this year, supporters of President Erdoğan, along with the president's own security, violently attacked a group of peaceful protesters outside of the Turkish ambassador's residence here in Washington, D.C. In this country, we do not attack those we disagree with. We do not start brawls to silence our detractors. In Turkey, President Erdoğan may be able to declare a perpetual state of emergency and change the constitution to better suit his desires, but Washington is not Ankara, and Massachusetts Avenue is not an avenue in Turkey.

The ongoing effort by the Turkish Government to intimidate Americans must end. The current detention of American citizens became all the more clear when President Erdoğan stated, "You have another pastor in your hands. Give him to us, and we will put yours through the judiciary. We will give him to you." Despite the strong, enduring alliance between our two countries, the United States cannot be expected to forego the rule of law in our country in order to extract some hint of it in another.

I hope we can come to an amicable solution on these matters, but to do so it's going to take more than relying on the trust and goodwill that has historically been built between America and Turkey.

It must require the adherence to the rule of law. I hope we move toward accomplishing that today.

Thank you, Senator Tillis, for the recognition.

Mr. TILLIS. Thank you, Congressman Burgess.

Congressman Hultgren.

HON. RANDY HULTGREN, COMMISSIONER, COMMISSION ON SECURITY AND COOPERATION IN EUROPE

Mr. HULTGREN. Thank you, Senator Tillis. Dr. Burgess, good to be with you. Thank you so much to our witnesses.

I'll be very brief. I want to hear as much as I can. And I apologize, Senator Tillis; I've got two markups over on the House side, so I'm going to have to leave in a few minutes.

But I am passionate about fighting for people who are suffering around the world, people who are being mistreated, and especially when we see governments that are doing this mistreatment. I'm such a proud member of the Helsinki Commission, but also proud to be co-chairman of the Tom Lantos Human Rights Commission. And so I want to do everything we possibly can.

That's my hope out of this hearing: To hear what we can do together—Senate, House, administration coming together to make sure that we bring these people home. Pastor Brunson is top of mind for me, but so many others that are suffering, that are wrongfully accused in so many ways, and these governments acting with what appears to be no accountability whatsoever. And we need to do everything we can to change that.

So thanks again, Senator Tillis and the Helsinki Commission, for holding this hearing. I look forward to working with all of you, but also with our witnesses to see what we can do to, again, bring these precious people home.

With that, I yield back.

Mr. TILLIS. Thank you, Congressman.

Our first panel features Deputy Assistant Secretary Cohen. He's been deputy assistant secretary for European and Eurasian affairs, governing Cyprus, Greece, and Turkey, since August 2016. He previously served in Baghdad as deputy chief of mission from 2014 to 2016, in Paris as the acting deputy chief of mission from 2013 to 2014, and as counselor for political affairs from 2011 to 2013.

Mr. Cohen, thank you for being here. You may proceed with your opening statement.

JONATHAN R. COHEN, DEPUTY ASSISTANT SECRETARY, BUREAU OF EUROPEAN AND ASIAN AFFAIRS, U.S. DEPARTMENT OF STATE

Mr. COHEN. Thank you, Senator.

Senator Tillis, members of the Commission, thank you for inviting me to testify this morning. Today's hearing is an important opportunity to reaffirm the abiding U.S. interest in and commitment to democracy, human rights, and rule of law in Turkey. It's also an opportunity to underscore the enduring strategic value of the U.S.-Turkey alliance, despite the current strains in the bilateral relationship and the challenges facing Turkey today.

Having spent the last 65 years as NATO allies, the United States and Turkey have deep, complex relations. With the second-largest military force in the alliance, a dynamic economy, and a population of 80 million, Turkey's critical position and regional clout have given Ankara significant influence over issues of core U.S. interest over the years, from Afghanistan to Iraq to the Balkans to Korea.

For example, from the early 1990s until 2003, Turkey facilitated the no-fly zone over the Iraqi Kurdistan region, allowing it to develop in peace and escape Saddam Hussein's tyranny.

In Afghanistan, Turkey was a major troop contributor to the International Security Assistance Force (ISAF), while also providing use of its airspace and allowing the refueling of U.S. aircraft on ISAF missions.

Turkey's an important partner in the Global Coalition to Defeat ISIS, and provides critical bases for United States and coalition military forces, from which we conduct precision airstrikes; carry out intelligence, surveillance, and reconnaissance flights; maintain combat search and rescue units; and resupply coalition forces.

We enjoy a robust and growing commercial relationship, a wide array of educational and cultural exchanges, and a vibrant foreign policy dialogue on issues ranging from Russian aggression in Crimea to limiting Iranian influence in the region to ending the war in Syria to the territorial integrity and unity of Iraq. We deeply value Turkey's contributions to global security.

The United States and Turkey need each other. As Undersecretary of State Tom Shannon has said, ours is not a partnership of convenience, nor of temporary interests; it's one of conviction, a time-tested alliance built on the enduring foundations of common interests and mutual respect. Our partnership is the result of sustained diplomacy, continuous high-level engagement between our governments to address challenges, explore opportunities, and move forward on a wide range of joint interests.

Since August, our presidents have had several phone conversations and have met on the margins of the U.N. General Assembly. Secretary Tillerson and Foreign Minister Çavusoglu speak regularly to consult on Syria, Iraq, and other issues. Our defense ministers have met twice since August. And of course, Prime Minister Yildirim visited Washington just last week to consult with Vice President Pence.

The United States-Turkey relationship extends beyond our mutual interests in stability and security in the Balkans and the Middle East. Both President Trump and President Erdoğan have committed to strengthening our trade and investment ties. Our extensive exchanges of students, scientists, and professionals ensure that our countries remain interconnected on a people-to-people level, and provide valuable opportunities for innovation and entrepreneurship, which are vital to our knowledge-based economies.

Ankara seeks further improvement in each of these areas of cooperation, and so do we. We will continue our efforts to develop constructive dialogue with Turkey in order to maximize the enduring benefits of our strategic alliance.

My remaining remarks today will focus on the United States Government's concerns about Turkey's protracted state of emergency, which has had negative effects on democracy and democratic institutions, on human rights, and on rule of law. Chief among those concerns is the security of and protection of human rights and fundamental freedoms for U.S. citizens in Turkey and locally employed staff at the U.S. Mission in Turkey, a number of whom have been arrested on dubious terrorism charges under the state of emergency.

As I highlight these concerns, it's in the context of Turkey being a longtime friend and ally, and with deep empathy and appreciation for the fact that on July 15th, 2016, Turkey endured a traumatic coup d'état attempt in which nearly 250 perished and thousands were wounded. The coup attempt was an evil attack on the Turkish nation and a tragedy for Turks, who bravely took to the streets to defend their democracy.

A few months after that, I stood in Turkey's Parliament building, the Grand National Assembly, and observed the destruction that Turkish Air Force F-16s had wrought on the people's house, in which all political parties sit. The Turks asked me to imagine the national trauma for us if such an attack were to happen here on our Capitol dome. It was a moment of profound impact for me. The Turkish nation was deeply shaken by the coup attempt, and remains so.

It's to be expected that Turkey would—and we support its efforts to—investigate and arrest those who directly participated or materially aided in the planning, preparation, and conduct of the coup attempt. The United States Government is carefully reviewing material provided by Turkey related to the Turkish Government's request that the United States extradite Fethullah Gülen, and will give similarly careful consideration to any new extradition requests related to the coup attempt. We again underscore our willingness to assist Turkish authorities in their investigation of the attempted coup and support bringing to justice those who participated.

But now, more than a year later, a restrictive state of emergency remains in place and appears to have been used expansively to target many Turks with no connection to the coup attempt. We were concerned to see Turkey extend the state of emergency for a fifth time on October 17th for an additional three months. The prolongation of the state of emergency has, in the view of the U.S. Government, negatively impacted Turkish democracy, rule of law, and respect for fundamental freedoms. We call on the Turkish Government to expeditiously end the state of emergency, release those not proven guilty of criminal offenses, and cease the seemingly indiscriminate prosecution of individuals—in many cases, individuals that appear to have been targeted because they criticized the government, its officials, or its policies, or have had contact with those who did.

There have been dozens of U.S. citizens detained or delayed by Turkish security services in some capacity since July 2016. Several U.S. citizens, including U.S.-Turkish dual nationals, remain in prison under the state of emergency, all facing what we believe are dubious terrorism and coup attempt-related charges.

Andrew Brunson, a United States citizen and Christian pastor who has lived in Turkey for nearly 25 years, has been in prison since October 7th, 2016. The outlandish charges against Mr. Brunson include gathering state secrets for espionage, attempting to overthrow the Turkish Parliament and government, and attempting to change the constitutional order.

The United States consistently calls for Mr. Brunson's release at the highest levels. President Trump, Vice President Pence, and Secretary Tillerson have all raised his case multiple times with their Turkish counterparts. On August 15th, Secretary Tillerson publicly called for his release during the International Religious Freedom Report rollout. Our embassy in Ankara continues to engage on this case, and provides consular services to Mr. Brunson and his family, meeting with him and his wife on a regular basis.

We remain deeply concerned about the detention of all U.S. citizens, including U.S.-Turkish dual nationals, who have been arrested under the state of emergency. We will continue to visit them when possible, raise their cases with our Turkish counterparts, and seek a satisfactory resolution of their cases.

In addition to the other U.S. citizens I've mentioned, it's worth pausing to note that Henri Barkey, a highly respected Turkish-American, has been subjected to a particularly vicious and groundless series of attacks in the Turkish media, which allege that he is the subject of criminal charges related to the failed coup attempt last year. I want to state clearly that there is absolutely no merit to the absurd idea that Henri Barkey, who has served with distinction in various expert capacities both inside and outside the United States Government, had anything to do with the coup attempt, or that he was acting to undermine the government of Turkey. Such accusations set back our relationship with Turkey, and undermine the credibility of the Turkish media as well as the Turkish judicial process.

Under the state of emergency, the government of Turkey has arrested two of U.S. Mission Turkey's locally employed staff on what we believe are specious grounds. Longtime U.S. Consulate Adana employee Hamza Uluçay has been in detention since February 23rd, 2017. On October 5th, Turkish authorities detained longtime Consulate Istanbul DEA local employee Metin Topuz. It appears to us that Mr. Uluçay and Mr. Topuz were arrested for maintaining legitimate contacts with Turkish Government and local officials and others in the context of their official duties on behalf of the U.S. Government.

The targeting of U.S. local staff, particularly those responsible for law enforcement coordination, raised our concern over Turkey's commitment to provide proper security for facilities and personnel, leading to Mission Turkey's suspension of non-immigrant visa services on October 8th. We have received initial high-level assurances from the government of Turkey that there are no additional local employees of our Mission in Turkey under investigation. We have also received initial assurances from the government of Turkey that our local staff will not be detained or arrested for performing their official duties, and that the Turkish authorities will inform the U.S. Government in advance if the government of Turkey intends to detain or arrest a member of our staff. Based on these preliminary assurances, we determined that the security posture had improved sufficiently to allow for the resumption of limited visa services in Turkey.

However, Mr. Uluçay and Mr. Topuz remain in custody, and we continue to have serious concerns about their cases. We'll continue to engage with our Turkish counterparts to seek a satisfactory resolution of these cases as well.

As a longtime ally and friend, we want Turkey to be the best democratic partner it can be. We have long supported—and we will continue to support—democratic development there, because we believe that respect for the rule of law, judicial independence, and fundamental freedoms are sources of strength and expand our potential for partnership. We will continue our constructive dialogue on the range of foreign policy and bilateral challenges, and we will also continue providing the assistance our imprisoned citizens and local employees need. We will not rest until all of their cases are resolved.

Members of the Commission, thank you for your attention today, and I look forward to your questions.

Mr. TILLIS. Thank you, Mr. Cohen.

I am going to defer first to Congressman Hultgren, then Congressman Burgess, so that they can get back to other business. If you don't know what markups mean, that means the chairman gets mad when you don't show up because they need a quorum to get going forward, which is one of the reasons why some of the Senate members may come in and out. Congressman Hultgren.

Mr. HULTGREN. Thank you, Senator.

And again, thank you for your service. Thanks for being here today.

I'll be very brief because, again, as I mentioned, I'm going to have to sneak out in a couple minutes, but wonder just briefly if you could talk a little bit more about what we could do as the Senate and the House, working in these specific cases. You talked quite a bit about Pastor Brunson. I'm grateful to hear that you've been able to provide consular service to him and his family there, also with the dual citizen NASA scientist Serkan Gölge. I wonder if you could talk a little bit more of what we can be doing to help, if anything, especially for Pastor Brunson, to get that release as soon as possible.

And then, as much as to the extent that the Privacy Act restrictions allow you to answer, I wonder how many U.S. citizens, including dual citizens, are currently detained in Turkey on coup-related charges. And do all of them have that same access to consular service? And is there anything else we can do for those people?

Mr. COHEN. Thank you for those questions, and let me start with the last question first. Because I don't have Privacy Act waivers, I can't be specific on the numbers, but we have fewer than a dozen. I would say several, including U.S. citizens and dual nationals.

The U.S. citizens were granted consular access quickly after they were detained. The dual nationals were not. Turkey does not consider dual nationals to be foreign citizens for purposes of consular protections. We consider anyone who has U.S. citizenship to be a U.S. citizen, and we pressed strongly for access for them. We were granted access last month—October—and we now, I believe, have access to all of the dual nationals who are in custody.

Similarly, some of the people in custody had difficulty getting access to legal counsel. After we pressed, we believe that they all now have had access to legal counsel.

And this gets to the first part of your question, what you all and what we all can continue doing to help. Engagement is critical. The fact that the Senate and the House have sent letters to Turkish officials expressing their concern is important. I would encourage you, if you travel to Turkey, to meet with Turkish officials and raise these issues; if you have the opportunity here in Washington to meet with representatives from the Turkish embassy, to do the same; or to meet with Turkish officials when they come and visit.

I should say I was in Ankara last month working on this basket of issues, and the approach that the Turkish officials had was a constructive one. They want to get past this problem as well. There are challenges on their side even for the people with the best will, because they also have a legal system that they have to navigate, and we have to be respectful of the limitations on them.

But I would urge you to continue your engagement, and also to continue comparing notes with the State Department and the Department of Justice as we go forward.

Mr. HULTGREN. Thank you. We will definitely do that, and please stay in touch with us if there's anything else that comes up that you think would be helpful. We want to do anything we can to come together to get this done. So thank you again.

Thank you, Senator Tillis and Dr. Burgess, for letting me jump in front here a little bit.

Thank you.

Mr. TILLIS. Thank you.

Congressman Burgess.

Mr. BURGESS. Thank you, Senator Tillis. And again, thank you for convening this hearing.

Secretary Cohen, thank you for your mention of Northern Watch. My youngest child was a young airman back in 2000 and was stationed at Incirlik and was part of that activity, and at least through the eyes of a 19-year-old at the time was always well-treated by the citizens of Incirlik. And he certainly enjoyed his time there.

You mentioned that you're now able to visit the people who are being held. Can you speak to the fact as to how you perceive, or your staff perceives, the people who are being held and how they're being treated? Is their physical condition good?

Mr. COHEN. The reports that I've seen indicate that their physical condition is acceptable. Again, I don't have Privacy Act waivers for most of them——

Mr. BURGESS. Sure.

Mr. COHEN.——so I can't get into the specifics. But the concern is with detention, not so much the conditions of the detention.

Mr. BURGESS. I understand.

Mr. COHEN. There have been some instances where people were detained in overcrowded facilities. In some cases they were able to get moved to less-crowded facilities. So there have been some improvements, and I want to acknowledge the cooperation of the Turkish authorities in that regard as well.

Mr. BURGESS. And in response to Mr. Hultgren's question, you gave an answer of less than a dozen United States citizens are being held. Does that include dual nationals in that number?

Mr. COHEN. Yes, sir.

Mr. BURGESS. OK.

Just to give context for people who may be watching and unfamiliar with the situation, how is the crackdown that's occurred in Turkey, how is that affecting the average Turkish citizen? How are they dealing with that?

Mr. COHEN. I think it's hard to speak about the average Turkish citizen. What I can say is that it has a chilling effect on public discussion about politics, certainly. It has had a chilling effect on the freedom of media, free expression, civil society organizations, all the points that were mentioned in the opening remarks by the members of the Commission. It's palpable when you're in Turkey. You can feel that the nature of public debate has been narrowed.

Mr. BURGESS. Very diplomatically put. What—and, again, forgive my lack of depth of knowledge of this—this state of emergency, is that in place at the order of the Turkish President, or is that the Turkish Parliament? Who has actually enacted that state of emergency?

Mr. COHEN. If you'll bear with me, I have a little fact sheet that I can go through.

Mr. BURGESS. OK.

Mr. COHEN. The government decrees issued under the state of emergency restrict suspects' access to legal assistance, allow suspects to be held without charge for up to a month and, in some cases, froze the assets of suspended or fired civil servants and their family members. Human rights groups documented some cases in which family members were held or subjected to restrictions on their freedom of movement in lieu of suspects who remained at large.

Under the state of emergency, detainees could be held without charge for up to 30 days, but there were numerous accounts of people waiting beyond the 30-day mark to be formally charged. Bar associations reported that detainees had difficulty gaining access to lawyers, both because government decrees restricted lawyers' access to detainees in prisons, especially those not provided by the state, such as legal aid lawyers, and because many lawyers were reluctant to defend individuals suspected of ties to the coup attempt.

A variety of sources reported instances of individuals wrongfully detained for ties to the coup based on poison pen allegations driven by personal or other rivalries. And the state of emergency itself is extended by the Parliament, proposed by the government.

Mr. BURGESS. Those restrictions of rights, those were applied to your two consular employees who were detained, or still are detained?

Mr. COHEN. I don't have the detailed information on that, but to the best of my knowledge they both have had access to their legal counsel. Hamza Uluçay is actually on trial. So his case has been brought to court on several occasions. I believe his next hearing is in December. So he has been formally charged. I'm not sure if Metin Topuz has been formally charged yet or not.

Mr. BURGESS. But still held?

Mr. COHEN. Yes, still held.

Mr. BURGESS. That 30-day requirement has long since passed. So under what authority has that been extended?

Mr. COHEN. Well, Metin was arrested on October 5th. So we're still relatively close to the one-month mark. And I can get back to you on whether or not the charges have been formalized.

Mr. BURGESS. And just, if you can—you may not be able to do this, but for those two consular employees, you mentioned assets have been frozen. Did that apply to our two consular employees?

Mr. COHEN. I am not aware of that.

Mr. BURGESS. All right. Thank you.

I realize this is asking for an editorial opinion. You may not be able or at liberty to give it. But what would have to happen for the Turkish Parliament to decide that it's no longer necessary to impose these restrictions?

Mr. COHEN. When I asked this of Turks—and I'll rely on what Turkish contacts have told me—they say given the breadth of the conspiracy that was perceived to be behind the coup, they believe they have more work yet to do before they end the state of emergency. And they cannot point to a time on the calendar when they believe that will be accomplished. To our mind, the number of people that have been swept up in the counter-coup is such, and the amount of time that has passed is such, that it looks to us like the state of emergency has exceeded its reasonable limits.

Mr. BURGESS. Have they—and, again, forgive me for asking something that may be just absolutely obvious—but have they identified the one, two, or three critical points that they need to see altered, changed?

Mr. COHEN. I think that's a question you'd have to address to the Turks.

Mr. BURGESS. OK.

Mr. COHEN. Sorry.

Mr. BURGESS. Thank you, Mr. Chairman. I'll gladly yield back to you.

Mr. TILLIS. Thank you, Congressman.

Mr. Cohen, to what extent is there any evidence to support the Turkish administration's position that there were those in the military associated with the Gülen movement that were responsible for the coup?

Mr. COHEN. The military participation in the coup is the most clear cut. It is indisputable that Turkish military officers used Turkish military hardware against state institutions and facilities on July 15th, 2016. So that's not an issue of dispute. What gets into a less clear category is who they were working with. And that is, I think, what is behind the scope of the purchase that we've seen.

Mr. TILLIS. I am interested in the current state of the rule of law, particularly in light of the April 17th constitutional referendum. Can you tell me a little bit about what the current state of the rule of law is in Turkey?

Mr. COHEN. Well, the April 17th referendum was to make changes to the constitution that transferred the state system from a prime ministerial, parliamentary-based system to a presidential system, putting more power in the executive. Those changes don't go into effect until 2019. So it's too early yet to be able to say how that will impact day-to-day life in Turkey. But I can refer you to the Venice Commission report, which suggests that Turkey will be losing a number of checks and balances in its system by implementing these changes.

Mr. TILLIS. To what extent do we really understand the mood of the Turkish people with respect to these changes, the current situation and future situation with these constitutional changes. Do we do any polling to get some idea of what the Turkish people think about this new change in leadership?

Mr. COHEN. Yes, we do, as well as some very well-known American institutions, like IRI, which is out there doing excellent work in Turkey. But the best indicator, I think, is the result of the referendum itself. It passed by the thinnest possible majority, sort of 51 percent, which suggests that some 49 percent of the Turkish public has misgivings about the changes.

Mr. TILLIS. Can you tell me a little bit about the charges against Mr. Brunson and Mr. Gölge? And in your own opinion, the reasons for their detainment and the charges brought against them, and shed light on your own view, or the view of the department, about the veracity of the charges?

Mr. COHEN. Well, as I said in my testimony, the charges against Pastor Brunson include gathering state secrets for espionage, attempting to overthrow the Turkish Parliament and government, and attempting to change the constitutional order. We do not believe there's any merit to any of these charges. We believe Pastor Brunson is an innocent, wrongly accused.

Mr. TILLIS. And on Mr. Gölge?

Mr. COHEN. We don't have a Privacy Act waiver for Mr. Gölge, so I can't comment on his case. But we also have not seen any indication that he's guilty of any criminal wrongdoing.

Mr. TILLIS. We have several questions that I want to submit for the record, but we'll move to the next panel in a moment. I have spent nine days in Turkey. I was there briefly for two days last year, but was focused on the refugee camps. But about 2011, I was there for about nine days and it was a very different Turkey. While the United States and several other countries were going through a serious downturn in the economy, there was just huge optimism in this country. We met with chambers of commerce. We met with a lot of Turkish families, spent time with Turkish families. That's when I learned you never tell somebody their food looks good, because you'll be eating most of what's on their plate. They're very good people. They were very optimistic. How would you view the mood of the Turkish people today?

Mr. COHEN. It's more tentative. As I mentioned in my remarks, Turkey suffered a national trauma. And the sense of that trauma permeates every aspect of society and it remains palpable today, or after the coup attempt. That said, the economy continues to grow at something like 5 percent, which is an enviable growth rate. And the Turkish economy continues to have great potential, including for American business. And I would reference the prospective deal between Boeing and Turkish Airways to sell some 40 Dreamliners, which is a deal worth over $10 billion that would employ 25,000 Americans. So there's a lot still to be accomplished in our bilateral economic relationship. And the Turkish people will benefit from continued economic growth, provided that it continues on the path it's on.

Mr. TILLIS. After that visit I hosted a delegation from Kayseri. I was in Izmir, Ankara, Kayseri and Istanbul. And my last city was Kayseri. And I spent a day with the mayor there, and other members of Parliament who came back to visit me in my then-capacity as Speaker of the House in North Carolina. And we were all optimistic about building great business relationships. I think the sooner we get past these sorts of things—which do not make me inclined to do anything with Turkey at this point in time—then we can get on to building those great relationships that I think would be mutually beneficial.

The last thing you mentioned about, in traveling to Turkey, meeting with officials there—one question that I had is, we met with several members of Parliament when we were in Ankara. Are there any members of Parliament who are openly sympathetic to our desire to have these people, who we think were inappropriately detained, released?

Mr. COHEN. I suspect there are. I haven't had any conversations since these arrests took place with any members of Parliament which led to this line of conversation. But it's an excellent question. I'll ask my colleagues in Ankara to see if we can find out.

Mr. TILLIS. I would like to do that. We had a very good discussion with several members that were there. And I would like to know that. Also, I'd like to know, if some of us were to travel to Turkey, would we be allowed to meet with the detainees?

Mr. COHEN. I hope so. That would be up to the Turkish legal authorities. But we have facilitated Turkish official visitors here having access to people that are incarcerated in the U.S. So it's certainly something for which we would advocate.

Mr. TILLIS. Well, we'll work with your office, because I have an interest in going there. And I would have an interest in seeking the opportunity to meet with the detainees and to also identify any members of Parliament that we may be able to meet with to really build a case for doing what I think is the just and right thing.

Mr. Cohen, thank you for being here. We've got a number of questions that the staff have prepared that I think would be very helpful and instructive to the Commission in terms of our path forward. So we'll submit them to you and would appreciate your response. Thank you.

I should have said this to begin with, thank you for your very long service to the country. And thank you for the very enlightening testimony.

Mr. COHEN. Thank you, Senator.

And thank you, Commission.

Mr. TILLIS. We will take a brief pause and transition to the next panel.

[Recess.]

Mr. TILLIS. Our second panel consists of three superb witnesses.

First, we'll hear from CeCe Heil, Pastor Brunson's U.S. attorney. Ms. Heil is executive senior counsel for the American Center for Law and Justice, specializing in public policy and global legal matters, including the United Nations. She manages the ACLJ's global partners and heads a team of lawyers handling cases in defense of life, protection of U.S. national security interests, and dealing with Islamic extremism.

Then we'll hear from Jacqueline Furnari, Pastor Brunson's daughter. Ms. Furnari is the 19-year-old daughter of Andrew Brunson. She has two brothers, Jordan and Blaise. She's currently earning her bachelor of science and business administration from the Kenan-Flagler Business School at the University of North Carolina at Chapel Hill. She expects to graduate in December 2017, with a concentration in entrepreneurship and operations management. Jacqueline was raised in Izmir, Turkey, where her father served as pastor of the Izmir Resurrection Church. In February Jacqueline married a Blackhawk pilot in the U.S. Army—which is why I'm convinced you're going to end up living in North Carolina after he retires from distinguished service, Jacqueline.

Finally, we're going to hear from Nate Schenkkan. A long-time Turkey expert who serves as project director for the Nations in Transit, Freedom House's annual survey of democratic governance in Central Europe and Eurasia. He previously served as senior program officer for Freedom House's Eurasia programs, covering Turkey and Central Asia. He was a lead researcher and co-author of two Freedom House special reports, including "The Struggle for Turkey's Internet," and "Democracy in Crisis: Corruption, Media and Power in Turkey."

Ms. Heil, we'll recognize you first for your testimony.

MS. CECE HEIL, EXECUTIVE COUNSEL. AMERICAN CENTER FOR LAW AND JUSTICE

Ms. HEIL. Thank you, Senator Tillis, Representative Burgess, for inviting me to speak before you today to discuss the case of our client, Andrew Craig Brunson, who's a United States citizen from North Carolina who is wrongfully imprisoned in Turkey. Pastor Brunson has lived peacefully in Turkey for 23 years, serving as the pastor of the Izmir Resurrection Church, and raising his family with no incident. But after the failed coup attempt in July of 2016, President Erdoğan started arresting anyone he deemed a threat, which included Christians. So on October 7th, 2016, Pastor Brunson was arrested as a threat to national security and detained, pending deportation.

However, Pastor Brunson was never deported. He still sits in a prison cell today, wondering if he's been forgotten, as today marks the 404th day of his detention. And as unbelievable as that may seem, given the current state of emergency and the subsequent emergency decrees from Turkey, all protections afforded in the Turkey constitution and with international declarations and covenants to which Turkey is a member, including the OSCE, all of those protections just disappear. And as a result of the rapidly diminishing state of law in Turkey, Pastor Brunson's file has been sealed, all of his visits from his attorney are recorded, and he can literally be held for up to seven years without ever being formal charged, completely destroying any ability to prepare an adequate defense, and obliterating all rights to due process.

So Pastor Brunson has remained languishing in a prison cell with literally no end in sight. And while Pastor Brunson has been in prison, he has lost over 50 pounds, he has lost precious time with his family that can never be replaced. And, worst of all, he has lost all hope, wondering why Turkey, a NATO ally and a country that he has loved and served for over two decades, has been able to hold held him hostage, an innocent United States citizen, for over a year.

Pastor Brunson's plight has caught the attention of hundreds of thousands of people across the world, and there's been an unprecedented amount of demands for his release from the highest level. As we've heard, President Trump has repeatedly demanded his release. Vice President Pence has repeated demanded his release. And Secretary Tillerson has demanded his release. And actually, most of you on this panel signed a bipartisan, bicameral letter that was sent to President Erdoğan, demanding his release.

And yet, on August 24, Turkey responds by levying additional ridiculous accusations against Pastor Brunson, these just as ludicrous as and disconcerting as the original. And still, not one piece of evidence has been presented to support any of the accusations against this innocent pastor. Pastor Brunson maintains his innocence and denies all the accusations, and reiterates that he has been in Turkey for the past 23 years for one purpose, and one purpose only, and that was to tell about Jesus Christ. So the question remains, why are they still holding him?

And perhaps President Erdoğan has given us the answer to that question in his recent demands for a swap of Pastor Brunson for either Fethullah Gülen or Reza Zarrab. So Pastor Brunson has literally become a bargaining chip for Turkey, proving that he is not a criminal to be prosecuted or convicted but a political hostage that Erdoğan wants to trade. Turkey is our NATO ally, and we should be able to say, give us our American, and they should give us our American. So we are asking you today to demand that Turkey give us our innocent American.

Thank you.

Mr. TILLIS. Thank you, Ms. Heil.

Jacqueline.

MS. JACQUELINE FURNARI, DAUGHTER OF ANDREW BRUNSON

Ms. FURNARI. Thank you for the opportunity to testify on behalf of my father.

Having grown up in Turkey, it has been so hard for me to understand the current state of events. My parents moved to Turkey in 1993, so that's where my brothers and I grew up. In fact, my brothers were raised there—they were born there. We even went to Turkish grade school because my parents wanted us to learn the language and feel comfortable in the culture. To me, it was home. My family, school, and friends were in Turkey. I grew up in the mix of Turkish and American culture, and loved seeing the beauty in both. On holidays, we sometimes hung a Turkish flag from our balcony, as our neighbors did. We loved and respected the Turkish people, and my parents were dedicated to serving them for as long as they could. My brothers and I used to joke that we would have to bring our future children to Turkey to see their grandparents.

As I grew up, I saw how my father poured himself into his work, and how willing he was to sacrifice his needs and wants for the sake of others. He believed—as I do—in a greater purpose in life, and actively lived out his life with the purpose of showing people the love and grace of God. He taught this message in the home, too. My parents' continued commitment to serving God and the people of Turkey was such a wonderful example for my brothers and me to see. We were truly blessed to be raised by such faithful parents.

I know my dad and his character as only a daughter can, and I know the charges against him are absurd. My father is not an armed terrorist trying to overthrow any government, my dad is a pastor who went to Wheaton College, then on to seminary, and got a Ph.D. in New Testament. He has selflessly served Turkey for 24 years now. Everything in his life is centered on his faith. For my family, who has loved, served, and prayed for Turkey and its people, seeing these absurd charges brought against my father has been an extremely painful experience. The past year of our lives has been filled with uncertainty, worry, tears, and countless unanswered questions.

My family kept assuming this situation would end soon. But it kept dragging on, month after month. My brothers and I didn't get to spend Christmas with my mom, because she was scared of what might happen to us if we flew into Turkey. I missed a last Christmas as a single woman with my family. I was about to transition into a different phase of life, and I wanted that one last family Christmas before things changed. In February I got married. We didn't want to get married without my parents present, but because my husband is in the military we could not postpone it. We had received my dad's blessing, but we felt so terrible about getting married while he was imprisoned. Neither of my parents were there, and I will never get that moment back.

For those of you who are fathers to daughters, I'm sure you would want to walk your daughter down the aisle. My father didn't get that. My husband and I decided to have a civil ceremony and to postpone our wedding until my father is home. I'm still waiting for my wedding. I'm still waiting to wear the wedding dress that I got almost a year and half ago. I'm still waiting for my dad to walk me down the aisle. And I'm still waiting for that father-daughter dance.

I'm graduating from college in December. My dad doesn't want to miss seeing graduate. He invested a lot in helping me find a career path. However, unless a miracle happens, I will be achieving yet another life milestone without my parents. In his letters, my father says that the hardest part of his imprisonment is missing out on being with his family. That is what he most wants. He has missed his only daughter getting married, and might miss my college graduation. He has missed helping my older brother make career choices and witnessing his accomplishments at Cornell. He has missed being with my younger brother who has so badly needed his dad and mom in the last year. These are the things that pain my dad the most, not being able to be with us.

In August, I took a risk and flew to Turkey to visit my dad and support my mom. I never really processed that visit because it makes me too emotional. I will never forget any moment of the day we got to visit. I remember hearing my dad's voice for the first time in a year as they brought him into the room. I remember how broken, tired, and desperate he sounded as he tried to fight to meet in a room where he could hug and hold us for the only hour he would have seen us the whole year. We sobbed the entire visit. It was hard to fit words in because the emotions were too strong and only led to more tears. It was difficult to see my dad so broken, so thin, and so desperate. He hated having his kids see him that way.

During my summer visit, he was already talking about how fearful he was at facing the cold winter in that poorly insulated prison. That he was already concerned about the winter in the middle of August shows how hopeless he was. And now, the cold that he feared so much has started. Seeing him in that much pain broke me. He's been changed by this experience. My whole family has been changed. In a recent visit with my mother, my father said: I plead with the Lord to release me by Christmas so I can be with our son in his last year in high school and at our daughter's graduation before she moves to Germany. But if I'm still here at Christmas, I'll thank God for sending Jesus to be born. If I'm still here at New Year, I'll thank him for helping me make it through this year. If I'm here on my birthday I'll give thanks for the life I've lived.

My father is now dealing with anxiety and depression, but he is handling his situation better than he was before. But we still want so desperately for him not to have to face another Christmas imprisoned. We want him to be home again, with his family. My family has suffered greatly because of these absurd and false charges. Please, make any and all efforts to secure my dad's release and bring him home for Christmas. He's been imprisoned falsely for far too long.

Mr. TILLIS. Thank you, Ms. Furnari.

Mr. Schenkkan.

MR. NATE SCHENKKAN, DIRECTOR OF THE NATIONS IN TRANSIT PROJECT, FREEDOM HOUSE

Mr. SCHENKKAN. Thank you. Senator Tillis, members of the Commission, it's an honor to testify before you today. I'm going to focus in my spoken testimony on some of the developments in rule of law since the coup attempt. I know we've covered some of this ground already. But I think, if anything, we may be understating how severe the crisis is in Turkey.

And I think that affects how we look ahead in the U.S.-Turkish relationship, and how it needs to be approached. My written testimony contains some more context about the state of rule of law in Turkey prior to the coup attempt. So I ask that you refer to that with questions on the matter.

Under the emergency rule for the last 16 months, some 150,000 people have passed through police custody on the basis of terrorist offenses, membership of armed groups, or involvement in the attempted coup. Of these, at least 62,000 have been arrested. One hundred and fifty-three journalists are in prison. More than 111,000 people have been fired from public service, which also means that they are placed on a blacklist, which largely prevents them from finding private employment.

The state has also closed and seized institutions around the country: 1,412 associations, 15 universities run by foundations, 162 media outlets, 2,271 private educational institutions, and 19 unions, 969 companies valued at roughly \$11 billion have been seized, 94 mayors have been removed from office and replaced by appointed trustees, 10 members of Parliament are in prison, two members of the Constitutional Court were removed from office and arrested, along with 37 personnel of the Constitutional court, 4,240 judges and prosecutors have been dismissed, 28 lawyers' associations or law societies have been closed, at least 550 lawyers have been arrested, and 1,400 lawyers are facing criminal prosecution.

As has been discussed, these emergency decrees under the state of emergency reduced very important protections for those accused or under investigation for crimes related to the coup attempt or membership of terrorist groups. These have led to increasing, and increasingly credible, reports of torture and forced disappearances in detention, which was a problem considered largely eradicated prior to the coup attempt in Turkey.

Regarding the constitutional referendum and the changes, I must respectfully disagree, slightly, with DAS Cohen regarding the effect on rule of law. Yes, the changes do not go into effect until 2019, but it is clear what that effect will be. The referendum changes increase the president's control over the judiciary. The president will have the power to appoint six out of the 13 members of the Council of Judges and Prosecutors, which controls the appointments of the judiciary. The remaining appointments will be made by the Parliament which is currently, of course, under majority control of the president's party. The oversight role of the Constitutional Court has been downgraded, as has that of the Council of State. In addition, of course, in this shift to a presidential system, the prime ministership is eliminated as an office and the president gains the power to appoint ministers.

It's within this context and the ordeals of Pastor Brunson, America's foreign service nationals, and tens of thousands of Turkish citizens, including leaders of civil society like Osman Kavala, that we need to understand this context of deteriorating rule of law. The executive branch in Turkey is constrained at this point neither by the balance of powers nor by the rights of individuals when it chooses to use politicized justice to achieve its political ends.

There will be three major elections in 2019 in Turkey. There will be nationwide local elections in March, parliamentary and presidential elections currently scheduled simultaneously for November. Each of these will be extremely important for President Erdoğan's goal of remaining in power and of retaining or, even better, strengthening his control over the levers of the state. We should not expect an improvement in the rule of law prior to the elections. It's not in President Erdoğan's interest, and it's not in the AKP's interest to have the system work more fairly or more justly at this time. Nor should we expect an improvement after the elections, unfortunately. If President Erdoğan and the AKP win, they will continue their effort to consolidate a paternal regime. If they lose even one election, they will have to tighten the screws in order to maintain power. This is what happened after the AKP lost its majority in Parliament in the June 2015 general election. So this problem of rule of law in Turkey is one that will be with us for a long time.

So let me say in that light a few words about United States policy towards Turkey in this area, regarding rule of law. The biggest problem is, first, that we treat it as something that we believe can be solved soon, or solved quickly. Of course, the first priority is returning U.S. citizens and protecting American employees, foreign service nationals, from persecution. But we need to recognize, no matter what the outcome is of these cases, this is a durable problem that will be with us. We need to recognize that the use of anti-Americanism and anti-Westernism by President Erdoğan and other political leaders in Turkey is driven by a domestic political dynamic. And nothing that the United States does is going to change that.

Instead of starting from a position of seeking to solve the problem of Turkey's political leaders taking anti-Western stances for their political gain, we need to define clearly first, for ourselves, what the United States core interests and values are in our relationship with Turkey, and then articulate policies to achieve those interests and values, including taking measures with Turkey to enforce them if they're threatened and violated. And I think there's been a lot of progress on this in the last year.

We also, though, need to keep an eye on the medium and the long term in Turkey, and what we want to see in Turkey. I believe the United States has a long-term, strategic interest in Turkey being a stable state, based on the rule of law, in which political and ethnic minorities enjoy fundamental rights, including the ability to participate fully in political processes. The United States cannot make Turkey into such a state. But this should be a key pillar for any U.S. strategic vision for the Middle East, and one that can be supported through measures taken now.

Some of those measures would include, first, using new instruments, including the Global Magnitsky Act, to sanction Turkish officials responsible for grave human rights violations. And of course, the congressional role in collecting those cases and forwarding them to the State Department can be very important. Second, I believe Congress should mandate funding for human rights defenders, civil society activists, and journalists in Turkey. Congress should create a special fund for those who support the country's future as a democratic, rule-of-law state.

Third—and this is where I think most of the progress has been in the last year—the United States can make clear that the rule of law in the United States and the rights of American citizens and employees of the U.S. Government are non-negotiable in the relationship with Turkey. If Turkish officials flout U.S. law, they will face criminal prosecution. We've seen this already, I think, in the Reza Zarrab case, which is one of the reasons why it's so important, beyond its implications, of course, as simply enforcing U.S. laws. The Van Hollen amendment is also an important step in this direction, reinforcing the importance of United States laws by underscoring that violations of our laws will affect U.S. support and cooperation with Turkey.

We also have to do the same regarding American employees and American citizens overseas. If the U.S. concludes that the detention of an American citizen is not based on a legitimate, criminal accusation, it should sanction officials responsible for their detention.

And this is why I support the Lankford-Shaheen amendment, and why Freedom House supports it. The U.S. must also stress that attacks on U.S. employees, including the offensive conspiracy theory regarding Henri Barkey and the imprisonment of foreign service nationals, will also result in the continuation of visa restrictions or other punitive measures, as needed. And I think Congress should be prepared to request sanctions against individual officials responsible for illegitimate detentions of U.S. employees.

There are no magic bullets for improving the U.S.-Turkey relationship. There are diverging values between these two allies. We should prepare for a very rocky short-term relationship and take necessary measures to guard the U.S.'s core interest and lay the groundwork for future improvements. It's my hope that the United States will stand with the many Turkish citizens working for democracy and rule of law in Turkey, and that circumstances will one day to improve to allow the bilateral relationship to return to a less tense basis.

Thank you.

Mr. TILLIS. Congressman Burgess, would you like to ask any questions before——

Mr. BURGESS. I have to leave, but thank you.

Thank you for your testimony.

Mr. TILLIS. Thank you.

Senator Shaheen.

HON. JEANNE SHAHEEN, COMMISSIONER, COMMISSION ON SECURITY AND COOPERATION IN EUROPE

Mrs. SHAHEEN. Thank you, Mr. Chairman.

Thank you all very much for being here and the work that you're doing. And, Ms. Furnari, I'm sorry I pronounced your name incorrectly, but no one should have to go through what your family has gone through. And I think all of us are in sympathy with your situation, and will do everything we can to try and address it.

Mr. Schenkkan, I appreciated the opportunity to work with you as we were working on the legislation with Senator Langford and on trying to restore some of the funding to address the efforts in Turkey around civil society. I wonder, in your testimony you said that we should not expect any improvement in the next few years. Can you talk about how matters could further deteriorate?

Mr. SCHENKKAN. I may, yes. What I think we should expect, unfortunately, in the short term politically, prior to the 2019 elections, is an expansion, in fact, of the prosecutions on conspiracy theory grounds around the state of emergency. I think it was asked in one of the earlier questions at what point the Turkish Government would consider their response adequate or to be finished regarding the coup attempt. I was in Turkey a month after the coup attempt interviewing various members of civil society, as well as politicians and others. At that time, the most fervent hope, in August 2016, was that the investigation of the coup attempt would remain within the appropriate framework, and confine itself to the coup attempt.

It was already clear within two weeks after that, that it was beyond that framework. And it has now spilled far, far, far beyond that. Unfortunately, under the state of emergency and under existing Turkish laws prior to the state of emergency, there are virtually no limits to how far a prosecutor, with a cooperative judge, may go in persecuting people for normal interactions with others. It's a guilty by association system. So the allegations currently being pressed against Osman Kavala, whose case I mentioned, a very prominent civil society leader, that involve Henri Barkey, former State Department official—these allegations in and of themselves can expand to include hundreds, maybe even thousands of people. Unfortunately, we face a very severe conspiracy theory scenario in Turkey.

Mrs. SHAHEEN. So, given what's happened, can you talk about how that's affecting the Turkish economy, and to what extent Erdoğan is affected by—I don't want to say a downgrade—but a worsening economic situation in the country?

Mr. SCHENKKAN. Yes. The economy is built on fragile ground. The Turkish economy had previously been orienting itself more and more towards an export-led approach, driven especially by cultivating new markets in the Middle East, in the Balkans, in Europe. Strained relations with Europe—that, again, President Erdoğan has cultivated for his own domestic political reasons—have begun to affect economic relations and investments coming from Europe. The strained relations with Russia that Turkey had previously engaged in—although now there's been a détente—had also contributed to undermining some of the bases for economic development.

So while DAS Cohen mentioned the very strong growth rate that Turkey currently posts, that's possibly based on some meddling with the numbers, according to economists. They changed how they calculate GDP recently. It also ignores the very high inflation right now in Turkey, which is well over 10 percent, and may be quite higher when we talk about food products which, of course, is the most important for the largest part of the population. So economic issues are very important for President Erdoğan. He's looking for ways prior to the 2019 election cycle to make sure that the average Turk, or at least his core base, feels that the economy is working for them. That requires some short term measures—as it has over the past several years—that may not be best for the long term.

Mrs. SHAHEEN. Thank you. I see my time is up.

Mr. TILLIS. If you have other questions, you're welcome to——

Mrs. SHAHEEN. No, go ahead.

Mr. TILLIS. I've been deferring to everybody to make sure you had an opportunity. Thank you for attending.

Ms. Furnari, you spent so much time in Izmir, right? How big is the congregation?

Ms. FURNARI. The church congregation? The size varies. Depends on the week, depends on the year, honestly. I would say, to the best of my knowledge, around 50 people. Some weeks lower, some weeks higher.

Mr. TILLIS. And in your time there, do you recall any time where you felt like you were being harassed or targeted by Turkish authorities, or your parents? Before the events that led to your father's detainment?

Ms. FURNARI. I would say there wasn't a feeling of that from Turkish authorities. But I think about six or seven years ago there was an attempt on my father's life by a gunman that came to the church. So I did have that sense of some risk and some fear and concern for my parents.

Mr. TILLIS. And Mr. Cohen testified that from the State Department's perspective, the conditions of your father's detainment were adequate. And then Ms. Heil and you both testified that he's lost 50 pounds in the 404 days that he's been in confinement. How do you reconcile adequate facilities with that outcome? And Ms. Heil, either you or Ms. Furnari. It sounds like the conditions are not the least bit acceptable.

Ms. HEIL. I would say the other situation that Mr. Cohen also referenced was being kept in a cell that was overcrowded—well, that was Pastor Brunson as well, because during a time of his detention he was kept in a cell that was built for 8, but had 22 prisoners in it. And of course, he's the only Christian. So, being kept up all hours of the night, not being able to walk outside, just the stress of not being able to sleep. And, again, being the only Christian—just the verbal abuse and the stress of missing his family have just led him to losing weight and being beside himself, with no end in sight.

Mr. TILLIS. Ms. Furnari, are you able to communicate with him, either through written correspondence or through the telephone?

Ms. FURNARI. Yes, I have been able to send him letters. Every once in a while, I get one from him. It's been very difficult for him to bring himself to write, though, because it reminds him of what he's missing out on.

Mr. TILLIS. Ms. Heil, it almost seems to me that maybe from the beginning of his apprehension that they viewed him as possible trade bait for someone here in the United States. Do you see anything that any reasonable person—have you seen any evidence that would substantiate any of their reasons for detainment that in a U.S. court would hold water at any level?

Ms. HEIL. No. In fact, his file has been sealed under the state of emergency, so no one has seen any evidence. So we have no idea. We have heard that there is a secret witness, but that's all. And every chance we've had, we've tried to demand concrete evidence. But no one has seen any evidence. And he has not been charged with any crime. He's still simply a suspect being detained.

Mr. TILLIS. Doesn't it defy logic that if the Turkish Government and Erdoğan had a compelling case against Mr. Brunson that they would want to put that forth to really communicate more effectively their basis for the illegal detainment?

Ms. HEIL. Certainly. If they had evidence to support their accusations of the crimes, you would think that they would go ahead and charge him and let the case proceed. But they have not.

Mr. TILLIS. Mr. Schenkkan, the referendum back in April of 2017—how have international observers judged the legitimacy of that referendum?

Mr. SCHENKKAN. The OSCE had a long-term observation mission in Turkey, as well as short-term observers, a full team. And their appraisal was very negative, in the measured terms, of course, that the OSCE monitors, ODIHR, typically uses.

Mr. TILLIS. Yes, so you've got a referendum that passed by the slimmest of margins, and then questions about the legitimacy of the referendum to begin with. Is that fair to characterize it that way?

Mr. SCHENKKAN. It's very fair.

Mr. TILLIS. You mentioned something, I want you to go back to it—I can't remember your precise words, but you were talking about the seizure of certain businesses that equated to the billions. Can you tell me a little bit about those businesses and why they would have necessarily been targeted?

Mr. SCHENKKAN. Of course. The Turkish Government's position is that the Fethullah Gülen organization, which they call FETO—which is not a name that the network uses for itself, but was provided by the Turkish Government in the last three years—included large business interests. And so businesses and businesses owned by affiliated businessmen were seized and handed over to the treasury, and they will be gradually auctioned off, again, in a process that is starting now.

In those auctions in the last 10 years, we have many examples of this auction process taking place when companies go into bankruptcy or are otherwise passed over into state hands. These auction processes are very frequently, if not universally, manipulated to ensure that especially strategic interests in areas like media wind up in the hands of parties friendly to President Erdoğan and to his government.

Mr. TILLIS. When I was in Turkey for that extended period a few years ago, I had the opportunity to meet with the ecumenical patriarch, Bartholomew. And interestingly enough, at that time he was pretty optimistic that things were getting better. What's the state of Christians in Turkey today?

Mr. SCHENKKAN. Well, I would have to say, first of all, that like we say in freedom of the press issues, the death of one journalist or the imprisonment of one journalist has a very severe chilling effect. The imprisonment of one pastor has an extremely severe chilling effect throughout a whole community.

Of course, the Orthodox and the Armenian communities in Turkey have special legal constitutional protections under the Lausanne Treaty, and in that sense also have a different relationship with the authorities than do Protestant Christians in Turkey. I think the main factor undergirding what's happened—which is affecting all Christian communities, including the official protected ones—is a very hard nationalist turn of the last three years; that has President Erdoğan embarking on a very anti-Western and very Turkish nationalist course in order to consolidate a different political coalition than the one that had backed him in the 2000s. He increasingly needs to marginalize and to push out ethnic minorities and religious minorities. And so the hate speech against them has certainly increased.

Mr. TILLIS. How much of Erdoğan's behavior, do you think, is rooted in his own belief of where he wants Turkey to go, versus just reading the political tea leaves and trying to maintain some order within the nation?

Mr. SCHENKKAN. It's one of the top questions among anyone interested in Turkey. I think it is principally about the political moment first and second about where he wants to go, because where he wants to go falls within a very wide spectrum, but where he wants to be when Turkey gets there—which is at the very top—is always the same. And so Turkey can get to a lot of different places with President Erdoğan at the top, and I think he's been maneuvering back and forth along different options as the political dynamics and the geopolitical dynamics change around him.

Mr. TILLIS. I did also want to ask you just briefly, you mentioned an amendment by Senator Van Hollen, I believe, and you also mentioned the effort on the part of Senators Shaheen and Lankford. What more should we be considering, beyond being supportive of those measures, as specific actions of Congress?

Mr. SCHENKKAN. Correct. Regarding the U.S. employees, foreign service nationals, I think we should be considering either widening Senator Shaheen's and Senator Lankford's amendment to include employees of the United States or adding a separate amendment for that purpose, because I think where we've arrived now—and it's correct, as DAS Cohen indicated in his testimony—that there has been some progress in the past couple of months, and in particular since the visa suspension, that that got the attention of the Turkish authorities and improved access to some detainees. It led to some changes regarding the potential detention of a third foreign service national.

That said, it hasn't led to the release of Serkan Gölge, of Pastor Brunson, or Metin Topuz, Hamza Uluçay. We're still just back at the beginning, which is not a good situation. So I think that it needs to continue to press forward. I think that's one.

I think, two—and this is more about the medium term and the longer term and how, I think, want to see Turkey as a stable rule-of-law state that is more inclusive and more democratic—there should be funding for civil society, for journalists in Turkey. The U.S. Government typically has not provided this kind of democracy and governance assistance for Turkey, except in very small ways—through the party institutes, through the occasional State Department Bureau of Democracy, Human Rights, and Labor call. USAID does not do work oriented inside of Turkey. There should be consideration for whether there should be a special fund or other mechanism for those who support a democratic rule-of-law state in Turkey.

Mr. TILLIS. Thank you.

Senator Shaheen.

Mrs. SHAHEEN. First of all, let me go back to the coup. Has there been any reliable information released from the Turkish Government about who was responsible for the coup, who in the United States we believe is objective and factual?

Mr. SCHENKKAN. Well, I can't speak for the United States Government or how they are perceiving.

There are multiple trials currently going on of varying relationship to the coup attempt. So you have some that are very much on the periphery and that prosecutors have claimed are connected to the coup attempt, like the case against Pastor Brunson or against others, the case against Osman Kavala or against the Amnesty International human rights defenders. All of these mentioned the coup attempt and implied that these people were somehow involved, but there was, obviously, no evidence.

There's another set of cases involving officers, involving military figures, as well as some civilians who are around the military bases. Those cases are taking place. There is a gradual buildup of evidence around what happened.

A couple of really severe problems with that.

Mrs. SHAHEEN. Yes, and I'm really asking not what happened, who were the responsible for the events of that period.

Mr. SCHENKKAN. Yes.

Mrs. SHAHEEN. I'm more asking is there any evidence around who was behind initiating that. The military—I haven't seen any-thing that suggests the Gülen network was actually responsible, but is there any evidence that's come out that would suggest that?

Mr. SCHENKKAN. There is evidence that there were members of the Gülen movement or network, some in the military and some who were civilians, who participated in the coup attempt. What their role was, whether they were the exclusive leaders or whether they were co-participants along with members of other factions in the military, is not yet clear, in my opinion. And this is, obviously, hotly, hotly debated right now.

Mrs. SHAHEEN. Right.

Mr. SCHENKKAN. Second—and I would say this even more strong-ly—there has been no genuine evidence offered of the coup attempt being directed from Pennsylvania, which is of course the implica-tion, from Fethullah Gülen.

Mrs. SHAHEEN. Right.

Mr. SCHENKKAN. That evidence continues to be circumstantial. It continues to be based on inference and not based on something that would stand up, I would say, in a U.S. court of law.

Mrs. SHAHEEN. And so what has been the impact of the recent reports that someone associated with the current administration, in the Trump administration, was meeting around the potential to ex-tradite or to send Gülen back to Turkey?

Mr. SCHENKKAN. Well, I think the biggest impact is that it dam-aged the clear message that the U.S. needs to send and has been working to send, that our system of rule of law is inviolable. The implication that there could be a side deal outside of the normal legal channels for the extradition or rendition of an individual who's legally entitled to be residing in the United States right now is very damaging. And so I think it is very important that—and I think the State Department has likely done this—we communicate that this is not the way to go about business.

Mrs. SHAHEEN. And how much does it undercut that message when we have the President embracing Erdoğan and not raising concerns about human rights issues in Turkey?

Mr. SCHENKKAN. I think it's a genuine issue that we want to make sure that human rights issues remain at the forefront of the agenda with Turkey. And we want them to remain there not only because they're our values and because this is what we stand for, but because this is in our strategic interest. This is an important part of how the United States wants to see events develop in the Middle East. Many of the issues that we see ourselves grappling with in Syria, in Iraq, as well as in the Balkans, have strong ties to the settlement and development of a democratic rule-of-law soci-ety in Turkey.

Mrs. SHAHEEN. Nate, Turkey has played an important role in NATO, and they have certainly been helpful in a number of the conflicts where NATO has participated. Can you talk about what, if anything, NATO might be able to do to address some of the rule of law and other issues that are happening in Turkey right now?

Mr. SCHENKKAN. Certainly, NATO remains principally a military alliance. It is a military alliance——

Mrs. SHAHEEN. Right.

Mr. SCHENKKAN.——and it has military tasks that it performs. The integrity of that relationship with Turkey has also been threatened by these developments, and that is one of the reasons why this is a strategic goal, to create democracy and rule of law in Turkey.

I think the NATO relationship will primarily be of use in this regard in that it is a means to communicate with Turkey how seriously the United States takes these issues.

Mrs. SHAHEEN. And the EU, I assume.

Mr. SCHENKKAN. Yes, of course.

To indicate that the kind of cooperation within NATO that Turkey will be involved in, and the level of Turkey's rank within NATO and what it has access to and where it falls within the hierarchy—because, of course, as such a large alliance, there is a hierarchy—that connecting these two will help. And I think it can be used in that way. I would not put on the table any kind of withdrawal or any kind of exclusion of Turkey from NATO, but——

Mrs. SHAHEEN. I would agree with that. I don't think that's helpful.

Mr. SCHENKKAN. Yes. But within the alliance itself, there continue to be very differing levels of cooperation. And I think making sure that when the United States says we value Turkey's strategic alliance and participation in NATO, what is understood by that is: and that participation will increase, along with improved cooperation on these other measures, rather than "and we will continue to participate no matter what, we will continue to offer you the same access no matter what," would be an improvement.

Mrs. SHAHEEN. Finally, I would just say that one of the things you point out—and I agree with this—is that we should recognize in the United States that Erdoğ an's anti-Western, anti-Americanism message is about his own interests, and that there's nothing that we can do that's going to change that tide. I would just qualify that a little bit, because you then go on to point out that, based on some of the proactive actions that we've taken in the United States, it has changed Turkey's behavior. And I would argue that we need to continue to look at those proactive ways in which we can change Turkey's behavior, and in some cases that means not only with incentives but also, as we've done through the Van Hollen amendment, try to provide some disincentives for Turkey, some penalties that they have to expect in terms of how we deal with them, and that that's very important for us to do. And as we look at how we deal with some of the people that they've imprisoned, we ought to be thinking about what ways we can invoke some of these incentives and disincentives to try and influence their behavior in terms of releasing those people who are improperly imprisoned.

Mr. SCHENKKAN. Absolutely. And I agree with how you understood or reframed my point. I think what I was trying to get at is we should not react on the basis of rhetoric and we should not react on the basis of trying to assuage or placate something that the Turkish Government is doing. We should act on the basis of these are our interests, these are our values, this is what we need to do to enforce them, because there's been a shifting and a perception from the Turkish side that maybe what were red lines are not red lines anymore. And those need to be enforced.

Mrs. SHAHEEN. Thank you.

Thank you, Mr. Chairman.

Mr. TILLIS. Thank you, Senator Shaheen.

Senator Cardin.

HON. BENJAMIN L. CARDIN, RANKING MEMBER, COMMISSION ON SECURITY AND COOPERATION IN EUROPE

Mr. CARDIN. Thank you, Mr. Chairman. I apologize for not being here throughout the hearing. We have a little tax bill in the Senate Finance Committee that we're bringing up. But I wanted to stop by.

Thanks, Senator Tillis. Thanks, Senator Wicker; Senator Shaheen, who is a key member of the Senate Foreign Relations Committee as it relates to this issue in Europe.

Our dilemma is this: Turkey is a very important strategic partner of the United States. Its location is critically important. It's critically important in regards to our campaign against ISIS, and it's a NATO partner. All of the above. But we ignore human rights and values at our own peril. If we don't package our policies in Turkey based upon respect for human rights of the Turkish citizens, it's going to be counterproductive to United States national security interests.

And it's been really challenging. It's been challenging under this administration because the Trump administration has not been clear at times as to American values. That makes it more complicated for us to stand up and say that we will not tolerate the mass arrests and the violations of dissent being tolerated in their country. So this is not an easy issue for us to figure out how we need to proceed.

But we have direct problems when Turkey is purchasing its military arms from Russia, which violates NATO uniformity and consistency, and violates our sanction bill with Russia. We've got to take action. You can't sit by and let those types of activities occur without the United States being strongly engaged on that issue.

I was in Europe this past weekend and had a conversation with our German colleagues in regards to Turkey. There is concern well beyond the United States on these issues.

So, Mr. Chairman, I don't have any specific questions for the witnesses, but I just really wanted to thank the Helsinki Commission for holding this hearing. I think this is extremely important. We've got to get this right. We need Turkey. I would suggest Turkey needs us. And their sensitivity on certain issues is, quite frankly, beyond our understanding. But we do stand for universal values, and they need to embrace a more open way in which we can have those discussions as partners.

Thank you.

Mr. TILLIS. Thank you, Senator Cardin.

Ms. Heil, we've had some questions about what more we can do as a matter of policy, and some of the amendments we've talked about already. But what more can we do to help you?

Ms. HEIL. As has been mentioned before even when you discontinue visa services out of Turkey, if there's any opportunity for negotiation, that Pastor Brunson never be forgotten as part of those negotiations.

As far as what will make Turkey respond, I think we would defer to the administration and the State Department because they have had direct negotiations and talks with Turkey, and they would be in a better position to tell you what they think would be helpful. But I would urge you to let them know how important this issue is to you.

Mr. TILLIS. Mr. Schenkkan, the discussion around the challenges that Senator Cardin did a great job of summarizing—on the one hand, they're an important ally in the fight on terror, and they're actually host to tens of thousands of refugees who are seeking refuge from the fighting in Syria. But the President has publicly asked for the release of the detainees. The Secretary of State has. What more should we ask of the administration beyond the posture and the public positions they've taken?

Mr. SCHENKKAN. I think that these issues of detention, especially the treatment of American citizens first and foremost, can be worked into other aspects of the relationship. I think, as my co-testifier was saying, there are many, many, many interactions with the Turkish Government on a daily basis, on a bilateral basis at the working level, of course. There are also many more medium-level and then high-level interactions. And I think that making it clear that this is not a matter of a single public statement or two public statements—that this will affect the NATO relationship, it will affect the security relationship—is an important thing to communicate to Turkey, and to communicate how it will affect that relationship going forward.

One of the things that we're seeing now regarding Turkey due to the detention of American citizens, due to the charges and conspiracy theories advanced about other Americans, is fewer Americans, especially those who would be most interested in working with Turkey—whether on a business basis or on a foreign policy basis or in other areas—being unwilling to travel there. And I think it's important that Turkey understand they're going to lose a large generation of people who would otherwise be very supportive and would be their allies if this continues.

Mr. TILLIS. Thank you.

Well, thank you all for your testimony. And, Ms. Furnari, I look forward to your father being at your ceremony.

Ms. FURNARI. Thank you.

Mr. TILLIS. We're going to hold the record open till the end of the week. We will have other members probably submit questions for the record. I have some that we'll be submitting to seek your input. But certainly, you have an invitation to contact my office, with a North Carolinian illegally detained, and all of the offices of the members of the Commission, to do everything we can to continue to provide support.

So at this point we will adjourn the hearing. But we will leave the record open through the end of the week. If you have any other additional information you'd like to submit for the record, we welcome you to do that.

And again, thank you again for your testimony and for being here today. Commission's adjourned. [Sounds gavel.]

[Whereupon, at 11:06 a.m., the hearing ended.]

APPENDIX

Prepared Statement of Hon. Thom Tillis

This hearing of the Helsinki Commission will come to order.

Good morning and welcome to this Helsinki Commission hearing titled "Prisoners of the Purge: The Victims of Turkey's Failing Rule of Law." I am honored to be chairing this hearing on behalf of Chairman Wicker.

As of today, an American pastor has spent 404 days in a Turkish jail without trial, without access to the evidence against him, the subject of a vicious smear campaign in the Turkish press, and facing life in prison on fabricated charges of being a terrorist and coup-plotter.

Elsewhere in Turkey, a Turkish-American NASA scientist has spent 480 days in prison—much of it in solitary confinement—on terrorism and espionage charges springing from the baseless testimony of a disgruntled relative and a bizarre compilation of circumstantial evidence, including a dollar bill seized at his parents' home.

Today also marks 253 days behind bars for a veteran Turkish employee of the U.S. Consulate in Adana who stands accused of terrorism for doing his job as he has for over 30 years, communicating on behalf of the U.S. Government with local community contacts.

These prisoners—Andrew Brunson, Serkan Gölge, and Hamza Uluçay—are the innocent victims of Turkey's collapsing rule of law.

With every passing day, the injustice of these detentions compounds itself. For the Brunson family next week: another Thanksgiving apart. For Kubra Gölge and her two young kids: another day away from their home in Houston. For Hamza, another inexplicable punishment for his dedication to the job he loves.

But the focus of this hearing is not personal—it's principle. Just as Andrew, Serkan, and Hamza have been victims of Turkey's failing rule of law, there are literally thousands more like them behind bars today.

Since imposing a state of emergency nearly 16 months ago, the Turkish Government has detained more than 60,000 people and fired or suspended upwards of 100,000 others from their jobs. The so-called "decree laws" authorizing these punitive measures do not establish any evidentiary standard for application thereby permitting wide-scale abuse as seen in the cases I've highlighted.

Of course, context matters, and the Turkish Government invoked its constitutional state of emergency provisions in the wake of the July 2016 coup attempt—an unacceptable and violent attack on the constitutional order of a NATO ally—an attack I unequivocally condemn. But the question is not *whether* Turkey has the right to pursue justice after such a national trauma—the question is *how* it goes about it.

The Helsinki Commission has called this hearing today to get to the bottom of the accumulating injustices under the state of emergency. As a participating State of the Organization for Security and Cooperation in Europe, Turkey has committed itself to upholding certain rule of law standards even under extraordinary circumstances. Among these commitments is the guarantee of equality before the law.

However, Turkey's commitment to this principle has been called into serious doubt. Just two months ago President Erdoğan proposed an outrageous swap involving Andrew Brunson—"a pastor for a pastor" in his words. If the United States would circumvent its rule of law to extradite a free man, Erdoğan suggested, then Turkey would release a wrongfully imprisoned one.

Let us be clear about what President Erdoğan proposed: this is not justice—this is ransom.

The United States should not expect—much less accept—this sort of treatment from a NATO ally. The harassment and detention of our consulate staffs has also overstepped the bounds of diplomatic conduct among partners.

I was glad to see the State Department in the past month impose some real costs for this behavior by suspending non-immigrant visa services in Turkey.

While the Department announced last week that it had resumed these services on a "limited basis" and received assurances about the security of our local employees, I hope that we are clear with Turkey that we will not accept anything short of true and timely justice for our detained consulate staff and our citizens behind bars. I also hope that we will not tire in advocating for the basic rights and freedoms of the thousands of Turks impacted by these sweeping purges: academics, mayors, legislators, journalists, and human rights defenders among them.

Let me conclude by saying that it is in the interest of the United States to have Turkey as a strong and reliable ally.

From strengthening NATO to fighting terrorism to resolving conflicts in the Middle East, we have important work to do together and we will be more successful if we can work as partners. The urgency of these tasks underscores the importance of resolving distractions and rebuilding the trust we need to achieve our common objectives.

And as always, our partnerships are strongest when they are rooted in shared principles.

We have two excellent panels of witnesses today to examine these topics. I will introduce the panels separately but I would like to say at the outset that I am especially pleased to have with us a State Department witness, Deputy Assistant Secretary for European and Eurasian Affairs Jonathan R. Cohen, to provide the Administration's perspective on these developments, U.S. policy toward Turkey, and the future of the bilateral relationship. I am also honored to have on our second panel Jacqueline Furnari, Andrew Brunson's daughter, from my State of North Carolina.

Our first panel features Deputy Assistant Secretary Cohen. He has been the Deputy Assistant Secretary for European and Eurasian Affairs covering Cyprus, Greece and Turkey since August 2016. He previously served in Baghdad as Deputy Chief of Mission from 2014-2016, in Paris as the Acting Deputy Chief of Mission from 2013 to 2014, and as the Minister Counselor for Political Affairs from 2011 to 2013.

Mr. Cohen, thank you for being here. You may proceed with your opening statement.

[Second Panel]

Our second panel consists of three superb witnesses.

First we will hear from CeCe Heil, Pastor Brunson's U.S. attorney. Mrs. Heil is Executive Senior Counsel for the American Center for Law and Justice, specializing in public policy and global legal matters including the United Nations.

She manages the ACLJ's global partners and heads a team of lawyers handling cases in defense of life, protection of US National Security interests and dealing with Islamic extremism. Next we will hear from Jacqueline Furnari, Pastor Brunson's daughter. Mrs. Furnari is the 19-year-old daughter of Andrew Brunson. She has two brothers: Jordan, 22, and Blaise, 16. She is currently earning her Bachelor of Science in Business Administration from the Kenan-Flagler Business School at the University of North Carolina at Chapel Hill. She expects to graduate in December 2017 with a concentration in Entrepreneurship and Operations Management. Jacqueline was raised in Izmir, Turkey, where her father served as pastor of the Izmir Resurrection Church. In February, Jacqueline married a Blackhawk pilot in the US Army.

Finally, we will hear from Nate Schenkkan, a longtime Turkey expert who serves as Project Director for Nations in Transit, Freedom House's annual survey of democratic governance in Central Europe and Eurasia. He previously served as Senior Program Officer for Freedom House's Eurasia programs, covering Turkey and Central Asia. He was the lead researcher and co-author of two Freedom House special reports including The Struggle for Turkey's Internet and Democracy in Crisis: Corruption, Media and Power in Turkey.

PREPARED STATEMENT OF HON. CHRIS SMITH

Good morning. We will hear today about the catastrophic break-down of the rule of law in our NATO ally Turkey and its personal consequences for several American citizens and thousands of Turks.

A key matter before us today is the Turkish government's apparent decision to hold hostage an innocent American pastor in order to extort political concessions from the United States. This "hostage diplomacy," as it has been called, is unacceptable when it is practiced by our enemies and appalling from our supposed allies.

Pastor Andrew Brunson was detained over a year ago on October 7, 2016. We know from Pastor Brunson's U.S. attorney, CeCe Heil, that the Turkish Government prepared an order of deportation on the day of his detention. The Turkish Government could have easily expelled him from the country then and there, bringing to an unjust close his 23 years of peaceful work in Turkey but sparing him indefinite detention. And yet it chose not to. Why was this order of deportation never executed?

Pastor Brunson's daughter, Jacqueline, will testify that prior to her father's detention the "worst case scenario for Christian pastors who were not nationals in Turkey was deportation." Again, why was Pastor Brunson not deported consistent with this precedent?

In February, I joined 77 of my colleagues from the House and Senate in writing to Turkish President Erdoğan urging him to release and then promptly deport Pastor Brunson. Nine months have passed without any response to that letter.

In the past 13 months that Pastor Brunson has spent in jail in Turkey, the President of the United States, the Vice President, and the Secretary of State, among many others, have interceded with the Turkish Government seeking his release. And yet to this day, he languishes in a punishing legal limbo without trial and without access to the evidence against him.

On September 28, President Erdoğan publicly suggested trading US-based Islamic cleric Fethullah Gülen for Pastor Brunson. Rhetorically addressing the United States, Erdoğ an declared in reference to Gülen "you have one pastor as well. Give him to us, then we will try him [Pastor Brunson] and give him to you."

With this statement, all doubt was removed as to why Turkey has failed to release Pastor Brunson for more than a year. Turkey is holding an American citizen hostage for a deal the United States will never accept.

Sadly, this is not President Erdoğan's only outrage against an American citizen. In May, during an official visit to the United States, Erdoğan's personal security detail—or, more appropriately, his goon squad—viciously attacked a group of peaceful protesters in broad daylight outside the Turkish Ambassador's residence in Washington, D.C. In the melee, 26-year-old Ceren Borazan from my home state of New Jersey was thrown to the ground, punched, kicked, and held in a chokehold by a Turkish bodyguard who threatened her life. Video footage shows President Erdoğan calmly looking on at the brazen violence. Even as 15 of his bodyguards have been charged in the US for the assault and the United States has cancelled handgun and ammunition sales to his security detail, President Erdoğan has never apologized.

I believe that we should examine the applicability of individual sanctions against grave human rights abusers in Turkey under the provisions of the International Religious Freedom Act and the Global Magnitsky Human Rights Accountability Act. These existing sanctions regimes, or a new tailored set, should be used to hold to account those responsible for the detention of Pastor Brunson and other cases of prolonged and unjustified detention in Turkey.

Thank you to our witnesses for their presence here and in particular to Pastor Brunson's daughter for her courage and candor in testifying today before the Commission.

Prepared Statement of Jonathan R. Cohen

Chairman Wicker, Co-Chairman Smith, Ranking Member Cardin, Ranking Member Hastings, Senator Tillis, and Members of the Commission. Thank you for inviting me to testify this morning.

Today's hearing is an important opportunity to reaffirm the abiding U.S. interest in and commitment to democracy, human rights, and rule of law in Turkey. It is also an opportunity to underscore the value of the U.S.-Turkey Alliance, despite the current strains in the bilateral relationship and the challenges facing Turkey today.

U.S.-Turkey Alliance

Having spent the last 65 years as NATO Allies, the United States and Turkey have deep and complex relations. With the second-
largest military force in the Alliance, a dynamic economy, and a population of 80 million, Turkey's critical position and regional clout have given Ankara significant influence on issues of core U.S. interest over the years. For example, from the early 1990s until 2003, Turkey facilitated the no-fly zone over the Iraqi Kurdistan Region, allowing it to develop in peace and escape Saddam Hussein's tyranny. In Afghanistan, Turkey was a major troop contributor to the International Security Assistance Force (ISAF), while also providing use of its airspace and allowing the refueling of U.S. aircraft on ISAF missions. Our long history of allied military cooperation also includes operations in Korea, the Balkans, and Somalia.

Apart from military affairs, we share many goals and concerns. Like us, Turkey wants to limit Iranian and Russian influence in its region; it supports a unified and sovereign Iraq; and it remains a partner in efforts to resolve the war in Syria. The Turkish government and people also deserve recognition for the enormous hospitality they have displayed in hosting more than three million Syrian refugees. We value Turkey's efforts to foster regional stability and its contributions to global security.

Turkey is an important partner in the Global Coalition to Defeat ISIS and provides critical bases for U.S. and Coalition military forces, from which we conduct precision airstrikes; carry out intelligence, surveillance, and reconnaissance flights; maintain combat search and rescue units; and resupply Coalition forces in closer proximity than possible from a U.S. base in the Persian Gulf. Turkish forces were critical in liberating key territory from ISIS along Turkey's southern border and degrading ISIS's lines of communication to the outside world. For our part, we underscore our commitment to stand with Turkey against terrorist threats, including the PKK and ISIS.

The U.S.-Turkey relationship extends beyond our mutual interest in stability and security in the Balkans and the Middle East. Both President Trump and President Erdoğan have committed to strengthening our trade and investment ties, as underscored by discussions in September on our bilateral Trade and Investment Framework Agreement. The recent proposal for Boeing to provide Turkish Airlines with forty Dreamliner passenger aircraft—a deal that, if finalized, is worth $10.8 billion and is expected to sustain 25,000 U.S. jobs—illustrates the potential of our economic relationship. Our extensive exchanges of students, scientists, and professionals ensure our countries remain interconnected on a people-to-people level and provide valuable opportunities for innovation and entrepreneurship, which are vital to our knowledge-based economies.

Ankara seeks further improvement in each of these areas of cooperation—and so do we. We will continue our efforts to develop constructive dialogue in order to maximize the enduring benefits of our strategic alliance.

Democracy, Human Rights, and Rule of Law

In my remaining remarks today, I would like to focus on the U.S. Government's concerns over Turkey's protracted state of emergency, which has had negative effects on democracy and democratic institutions, on human rights, and on rule of law. Chief among those concerns is the security of and protection of human rights and fundamental freedoms for U.S. citizens in Turkey and locally employed staff at the U.S. Mission in Turkey, a number of whom have been arrested on dubious terrorism charges under the state of emergency.

As I highlight these concerns, it is in the context of Turkey being a longtime friend and Ally, and with deep empathy and appreciation for the fact that on July 15, 2016, Turkey endured a traumatic coup d'état attempt. We continue to support Turkey's efforts to bring to justice those responsible for the failed coup. It is in the national interest of both the United States and Turkey for Turkey to be stable, democratic, and prosperous. We continue to support Turkey's democratic development and vigorously encourage application of the rule of law, including due process, transparency, and judicial independence.

The July 2016 attempted coup, in which nearly 250 perished and thousands were wounded, was an evil attack on democracy and a tragedy for Turks, who bravely took to the streets to defend their democracy. A few months later, I stood in Turkey's parliament building, the Grand National Assembly, and observed the destruction that Turkish Air Force F-16s had wrought on the people's house, in which all political parties sit. The Turks asked me to imagine the national trauma if such an attack had happened here on our Capitol dome. The Turkish nation was shaken by the coup attempt and remains so.

It is to be expected that Turkey would—and we support its efforts to—investigate and arrest those who directly participated or materially aided in the planning, preparation, and conduct of the coup attempt. The U.S. Government is carefully reviewing material provided by Turkey related to the Turkish Government's request that the United States extradite Fethullah Gü len and will give similarly careful consideration to any new extradition requests related to the coup attempt. We again underscore our willingness to assist Turkish authorities in their investigation of the attempted coup and support bringing to justice those who participated.

Now, more than one year later, a restrictive state of emergency remains in place and appears to have been used expansively to target many Turks with no connection to the coup attempt. We were concerned to see Turkey extend the state of emergency for a fifth time on October 17 for an additional three months.

The prolongation of the state of emergency has, in the view of the U.S. Government, negatively impacted Turkish democracy, rule of law, and respect for fundamental freedoms. The Turkish government has expropriated nearly one thousand private businesses and dismissed well over 100,000 from their jobs. Tens of thousands have been arrested on terror-related charges. Authorities have imprisoned a growing number of opposition lawmakers, journalists, leading intellectuals, academics, civil society activists, and respected human rights defenders—including respected philanthropist Osman Kavala, Amnesty International Turkey's Chairman Taner Kilic, and its recently released Director Idil Eser. We call on the Turkish government to expeditiously end the state of emergency, release those not proven guilty of criminal offenses, expedite due process for dismissed civil servants, and cease the seemingly indiscriminate prosecution of individuals—in many cases, individuals that appear to have been targeted because they criticize the government, its officials, or its policies, or have had contact with those who did.

As the Department of State has made clear in numerous press statements since the coup attempt, these detentions and prosecutions, often with little evidence, transparency, or effective mechanism for redress, undermine confidence in the rule of law in Turkey. The U.S. Mission in Turkey is closely following these cases, monitoring trials, engaging with civil society leaders, and working with like-minded partners to underscore the importance of respect for rule of law and individual rights, including fair trial guarantees. These rights are enshrined in the Turkish Constitution and are part of Turkey's international obligations and commitments.

Additionally, we have seen a worrisome diminishment in freedom of the media and freedom of expression. Detentions of journalists under emergency rule have effectively silenced most independent media, most notably via the trial of 17 journalists and media executives—four of whom remain in custody—for Turkey's leading independent newspaper, Cumhuriyet. As we have expressed publicly and to the Turkish government on numerous occasions, curbs on freedom of expression, freedom of assembly and association, and other fundamental freedoms erode the foundations of democratic society, and are impediments to re-establishing the social and legal underpinnings of state and public security. Turkey benefits from having more engaged voices, not fewer—even voices it may find controversial or uncomfortable.

American Citizen Detentions

One of the Department of State's highest priorities is assisting U.S. citizens abroad and providing all possible consular services to U.S. citizens in need.

There have been dozens of U.S. citizens detained or delayed by Turkish security services in some capacity since July 2016. Several U.S. citizens, including U.S.-Turkish dual nationals, remain in prison under the state of emergency, all facing dubious terrorism and coup attempt-related charges.

As there is no international obligation to grant consular access to dual nationals, and as Turkey does not consider U.S.-Turkish dual nationals to be U.S. citizens for the purposes of consular notification, we were long denied access to our dual nationals detained under state of emergency provisions. After sustained U.S. Government engagement, the Government of Turkey for the first time granted us consular access to these dual nationals in mid-October of this year. High-level conversations continue to enhance cooperation and are yielding progress on a range of legal issues.

Andrew Brunson, a U.S. citizen and Christian pastor who has lived in Turkey for nearly 25 years, has been in prison since October 7, 2016. Of the U.S. citizens now detained in Turkey under the state of emergency, he has been held the longest without a judicial hearing. The outlandish charges against Mr. Brunson include gathering state secrets for espionage, attempting to overthrow the Turkish parliament and government, and attempting to change the constitutional order. The United States consistently calls for Mr. Brunson's release at the highest levels—President Trump, Vice President Pence, and Secretary Tillerson have all raised his case multiple times with their Turkish counterparts. On August 15, Secretary Tillerson publicly called for his release during the International Religious Freedom Report rollout. Our Embassy in Ankara continues to engage on this case and provide consular services to Mr. Brunson and his family, meeting with him and his wife on a regular basis.

We remain deeply concerned about the detention of all U.S. citizens, including U.S.-Turkish dual nationals, who have been arrested under the state of emergency. We will continue to visit them when possible, raise their cases with our Turkish counterparts, and seek a satisfactory resolution of their cases.

Locally Employed Staff and Visa Suspension

Under the state of emergency, the Government of Turkey arrested two of U.S. Mission Turkey's locally employed staff on what we believe are specious grounds. Longtime U.S. Consulate Adana employee Hamza Uluçay has been in detention since February 23, 2017. On October 5, Turkish authorities detained longtime Consulate Istanbul DEA local employee Metın Topuz. A number of other locally employed staff have come under investigation, and one employee's wife and daughter were held in jail without charges for nine days last month. The Turkish government has leveled flimsy terrorism charges against both Mr. Uluçay and Mr. Topuz. It appears they were arrested for maintaining legitimate contacts with government officials and others in the context of their official duties on behalf of the U.S. Government. We have and will continue to push for their release.

The targeting of U.S. local staff, particularly those responsible for law enforcement coordination, raised our concern over Turkey's commitment to providing proper security for our diplomatic and consular facilities and personnel, leading to Mission Turkey's suspension of non-immigrant visa services on October 8. We have received initial high-level assurances from the Government of Turkey that there are no additional local employees of our Mission in Turkey under investigation. We have also received initial assurances from the Government of Turkey that our local staff will not be detained or arrested for performing their official duties, and that Turkish authorities will inform the U.S. Government in advance if the Government of Turkey intends to detain or arrest a member of our local staff.

Based on these preliminary assurances, we determined the security posture had improved sufficiently to allow for the resumption of limited visa services in Turkey. However, Mr. Uluçay and Mr. Topuz remain in custody and we have serious concerns about their cases. We will continue to engage with our Turkish counterparts to seek a satisfactory resolution of these cases, as well.

No Linkage Between Cases in U.S., Turkey

Some in the Turkish government have made efforts to equate cases involving our local staff with the arrest in the United States of a senior executive of Turkey's state-owned Halk Bank. The two situations and contexts are very different and the U.S. Government strongly objects to any effort to link them. The executive, Mehmet Hakan Atilla, has been charged with conspiring to evade U.S. sanctions against Iran. Our employees were arrested on terrorism charges based on contact, in the course of their official duties, with Turkish officials whom the Turkish state now finds unpalatable.

Enduring U.S.-Turkey Relations

As a longtime Ally and friend, we want Turkey to be the best democratic partner it can be. We have long supported—and will continue to support—democratic development there, because we believe that respect for the rule of law, judicial independence, and fundamental freedoms are sources of strength and expand our potential for partnership. We will also continue providing the assistance our imprisoned citizens and local employees need, and will not rest until all of their cases are resolved.

Members of the Commission, thank you for your attention today. I look forward to answering your questions.

Prepared Statement of CeCe Heil

Chairman Wicker, Chairman Smith, Ranking Member Cardin, Ranking Member Hastings, and distinguished Commissioners, thank you for inviting me to speak before you today and for the opportunity to highlight a case that warrants your careful attention.

Andrew Craig Brunson is a United States citizen and pastor from North Carolina. For over 23 years, Pastor Brunson has lived peacefully in Turkey, serving as pastor of the Izmir Resurrection church, and raising his family without incident. Then, on October 7, 2016, Pastor Brunson arrived home to find a written summons to report with his passport to a local police station. Believing the summons was related to his routine application for a renewal of his residence visa, Pastor Brunson promptly reported to the Izmir police, only to be arrested and informed that an order of deportation had been entered against him, as he had suddenly been deemed a threat to national security. He was to be held in the Harmandali Detention Centre pending deportation. However, Pastor Brunson was never deported; instead he remains unjustly incarcerated in Turkey, wondering if he has been forgotten, as today marks the 404th day of his detention. And just what crime has Pastor Brunson committed? He literally has no idea, and has yet to be charged with any crime.

As unbelievable as that may seem, under the current State of Emergency in Turkey, and subsequent emergency decrees, all protections afforded by Turkey's Constitution, or in International Declarations and Covenants, including those contained in the Organization for Security and Co-operation in Europe (OSCE), of which Turkey is a member, just disappear. Despite President Erdoğan's recent public declarations that Turkey is indeed a state of laws, the fact that he has the sole power to change the law at his whim, and remove any obligation to be bound by it, wholly undermines those claims. As a result of the rapidly diminishing rule of law, Pastor Brunson's file has been sealed, all visits from his attorney are recorded, and he can be held without any formal charges for up to 7 years, completely destroying any ability to prepare an adequate defense, and obliterating all rights to due process.

Accordingly, after his arrest, Pastor Brunson continued to remain in detention at the Harmandali Centre, and was denied access to an attorney until December 9th, 2016—over two months later—when he was transferred in the middle of the night to a high security prison in Izmir. At that time, he was informed that he was being detained as a suspect, although evidence had yet to be gathered, on the absurd grounds of Membership in an Armed Terrorist Organization. The ensuing months were filled with multiple appeals contesting his detention, which cited the legal deficiencies of such a decision, and all of which were summarily denied, even though no evidence has been set forth to substantiate any crime. So, Pastor Brunson has remained, languishing in a prison cell with no end in sight.

While in prison, Pastor Brunson has lived under inhumane conditions, and has spent extended periods of time in a cell meant for eight people, but which at times has held as many as 22 prisoners, of which Pastor Brunson is always the only Christian. During his incarceration, Pastor Brunson has lost over 50 pounds, he has lost precious time with his family that can never be replaced, but worst of all, he has lost hope, wondering why Turkey, a NATO ally and a country he loves and has served for over 2 decades, has been able to hold held him hostage, an innocent United States citizen, for over a year.

During this ordeal, Pastor Brunson's plight has caught the attention of hundreds of thousands of people around the world and there have been an unprecedented amount of high level demands for Pastor Brunson's release. And yet, on August 24, 2017, the Turkish Government decided to levy new and additional accusations against Pastor Brunson, these just as ludicrous as and even more disconcerting than the original. They include, Political or Military Espionage, Attempting to overthrow the Government, Attempting to overthrow the Turkish Grand National Assembly, and Attempting to overthrow the Constitutional Order, with the last three not only carrying aggravated life sentences, but requiring that the accused used force and violence. And once again, no evidence has been put forth to substantiate such ridiculous accusations. Pastor Brunson has and continues to adamantly maintain his innocence and deny all the accusations. He has reiterated that his sole purpose for being in Turkey for the past 23 years was "for one purpose only. To tell about Jesus Christ." He has further stated that he has "done this openly, in front of the government." And so the question remains, why are they still holding him?

Perhaps President Erdoğan himself answered this question when he recently demanded a swap of Pastor Brunson for Fethullah Gülen, the cleric Erdoğan blames for the failed coup attempt in July of last year. So, Pastor Brunson's incarceration has simply become a bargaining chip for Turkey. However, I would submit that President Erdoğan has mistakenly been led to believe that Pastor Brunson's value lies simply as a pawn in a swap. In reality, Pastor Brunson's greatest value to Turkey lies in President Erdoğan's approval of his immediate release back to the U.S. as a sign of good will, and as a major step toward restoring amicable relations between Turkey and the United States; an invaluable move with immeasurable and long-lasting benefits. We should use every effort to make sure that President Erdoğan gets that message.

PREPARED STATEMENT OF JACQUELINE FURNARI

Chairman Wicker, Chairman Smith, Ranking Member Cardin, Ranking Member Hastings, and distinguished Commissioners, thank you for the opportunity to testify on behalf of my father.

Having grown up in Turkey, it has been so hard for me to understand the current state of events. My parents moved to Turkey in 1993, so that's where my brothers and I grew up. In fact, my brothers were born there. We even went to Turkish grade school because my parents wanted us to learn the language and feel comfortable in the culture. To me, it was home. My family, school, and friends were in Turkey. I grew up in the mix of Turkish and American culture, and loved seeing the beauty in both. On holidays, we sometimes hung a Turkish flag from our balcony, as our neighbors did. We loved and respected the Turkish people, and my parents were dedicated to serving the Turkish people for as long as they could. My brothers and I used to joke that we would have to bring our future children to Turkey to see their grandparents.

As I grew up, I saw how my father poured himself into his work, and how willing he was to sacrifice his needs and wants for the sake of others. He believed—as I do—in a greater purpose in life, and actively lived out his life with the purpose of showing people the love and grace of God. He taught this message in the home, too. Their continued commitment to serving God and the people of Turkey was such a wonderful example for my brothers and me to see. We were truly blessed to be raised by such faithful parents.

I know my dad and his character, as only a daughter can, and I know the charges against him are absurd. My father is not an armed terrorist trying to overthrow any government, my father is a pastor who went to Wheaton College, then on to seminary, and got a Ph.D. in New Testament. He has selflessly served Turkey for 24 years now. Everything in his life is centered on his faith. For my family, who has loved, served, and prayed for Turkey and its people, seeing these absurd charges brought against my father has been an extremely painful experience.

Previously, the worst case scenario for Christian pastors, who were not nationals, in Turkey was deportation, which is why I never could have guessed my father would be imprisoned there for over a year. This is unheard of. My family has been shocked and deeply hurt during the past year. The past year of our lives has been filled with uncertainty, worry, tears, and countless unanswered questions.

I didn't even know when my parents were detained in October last year. I only found out several days after the fact because they took their phones and did not let them contact anyone. For what felt like weeks, I was in a state of panic. This hadn't happened before. I couldn't find out any information about what the charges were. There was no communication for two weeks, although we tried desperately to find out any information. Then, my mother was released. I called her the moment I got her message. I will never forget how shocked and brokenhearted she was because my father was still detained and no one knew why.

My family kept assuming this situation would end soon. But it kept dragging on, month after month. My brothers and I didn't get to spend Christmas with my mom because she was scared of what might happen to us if we flew into Turkey. I missed a last Christmas as a single woman with my family. I was about to transition into a different phase of life, and I wanted that one last family Christmas before things changed.

In February I got married. We didn't want to get married without my parents present, but because my husband is in the military, we could not postpone it. We had received my father's blessing, but we felt so terrible about getting married while he was imprisoned. Neither of my parents were present when I got married. I will never get that moment back. For those of you who are fathers to daughters, I'm sure you would want to walk your daughter down the aisle. My father didn't get that. I didn't get that. My husband and I decided to have a civil ceremony and to postpone our wedding ceremony until my father is home. I'm still waiting for my wedding. I'm still waiting to wear the wedding dress that I got almost a year and half ago. I'm still waiting for my dad to walk me down the aisle. I'm still waiting for that father-daughter dance.

I'm graduating from college in December. My dad doesn't want to miss seeing me graduate. He invested a lot in helping me find a career path. However, unless a miracle happens, I will be achieving yet another life milestone without my parents.

In his letters, my father says that the hardest part of his imprisonment is missing out on being with his family. That is what he most wants. He has missed his only daughter getting married, and might miss my college graduation. He has missed helping my older brother make career choices and witnessing his accomplishments at Cornell. He has missed being with my younger brother who has so badly needed his dad and mom in the last year. These are the things that pain my dad the most, not being able to be with us.

In August, I took a risk and flew to Turkey to visit my father and support my mother. I never really processed that visit because it makes me too emotional. I will never forget any moment of the day we got to visit. I remember hearing my dad's voice for the first time in a year as they brought him into the room. I remember how broken, tired, and desperate he sounded as he tried to fight to meet in a room where he could hug and hold us for the only hour he would have seen us the whole year. We sobbed the entire visit. It was hard to fit words in because the emotions were too strong and only led to more tears. It was hard to see my father so broken, so thin, so desperate. He hated having us kids see him that way.

During my summer visit, he was already talking about how fearful he was of facing the cold winter in that poorly insulated prison. That he was already concerned about the winter in the middle of August shows how hopeless he was. And now, the cold that he feared so much has started. My father is now dealing with anxiety and depression. Seeing him in that much pain broke me. He's been changed by this experience. My whole family has been changed.

In a recent visit with my mother, my father said "I plead with the Lord to release me by Christmas so I can be with our son in his last year in high school and at our daughter's graduation before she moves to Germany. But if I'm still here at Christmas, I'll thank God for sending Jesus to be born. If I'm still here at New Year, I'll thank him for helping me make it through this year. If I'm here on my birthday, I won't be like Job and curse the day I was born. I'll give thanks for the life I've lived." My father is handling his situation better than he was before. But we still want so desperately for him not to have to face Christmas imprisoned again. We want him to be home again, with his family.

My family has suffered greatly because of these absurd and false charges. Please, make any and all efforts to secure my father's release and bring him home for Christmas. He's been falsely imprisoned for far too long.

PREPARED STATEMENT OF NATE SCHENKKAN

We have heard today already about some of the ways in which the erosion of the rule of law in Turkey has entrapped and endangered Americans. I will speak today about the state of the rule of law in Turkey, what to expect in the next few years, and how the U.S. can rebalance its relationship with Turkey around the rule of law. Modern Turkey's institutions have always been weak in terms of democratic accountability and the protection of human rights.

Modern Turkey's legal and constitutional tradition places greater priority on the unity of the nation and the integrity of the state than on the rights of the individual and the separation of powers. There was a brief window in the 2000s when Turkey sought to align with European Union standards, during which Turkey made a number of cardinal reforms to strengthen the independence of institutions and protect human rights, but that was followed by a sustained attack on the rule of law and democratic institutions for much of the last decade.

The partnership between the ruling AKP and the Gülen movement that became entrenched during the 2000s did severe damage to the judiciary through instrumentalized trials of Kurdish activists, the military, media, and secular elites. After the AKP and the Gülen movement fell out in late 2013, the government turned on the judiciary in order to eliminate its former allies.

Two changes stand out:

- In February 2014, the government amended the law on the High Council of Judges and Prosecutors (HSYK), which controls appointments to the judiciary, to strengthen the Minister of Justice's role in the Council, including by reassigning members of the Council. This reversed key reforms to ensure the independence of the judiciary that the government had supported in 2010.
- In June 2014, the government established a new institution called "peace judgeships" (*Sulh Ceza Hakimlikleri*) with responsibility for so-called "protective measures," including approving pretrial detentions, and removing content from the internet and closing internet websites. These new peace judgeships lack appropriate mechanisms for appeal and oversight, and have been a major factor in the increased use of pretrial detention and internet blocking in the period after 2014.

Following the coup attempt of July 2016, the government has used the state of emergency to eradicate what it perceives as sources of opposition, to subordinate the judiciary even further, and to dismantle rule of law protections.

Turkey has been under emergency rule for 16 months. During this time:

- Some 150,000 people have passed through police custody on the basis of terrorist offenses, membership of armed groups, or involvement in the attempted coup. Of those, at least 62,000 have been arrested.
- 153 journalists are in prison.
- More than 111,000 people have been fired from public service through emergency decrees without adequate due process pro-

tections. They are effectively blacklisted, which means they will be unable to find public employment and are evicted from public housing; many if not most will not be able to find private employment, either.

- The state has also closed and seized institutions around the country:
  - 1,412 associations have been closed
  - 15 universities run by foundations have been closed
  - 162 media outlets have been closed, including 6 news agencies, 48 newspapers, 20 magazines, 31 radio stations, 28 TV stations, and 29 publishing houses
  - 2,271 private educational institutions have been closed
  - 19 unions have been closed
  - 969 companies valued at approximately $11 billion have been seized
  - 94 mayors have been removed and replaced by "trustees" appointed by Ankara
  - 10 members of parliament are in prison, including the co-leaders of the second-largest opposition party
- 2 members of the Constitutional Court were removed from their positions and arrested, along with 37 personnel of the court.
- 183 staff were dismissed from the Supreme Court; 91 from the Council of State; and 153 from the General Accounting Bureau
- 4,240 judges and prosecutors have been dismissed (2956 judges and 1284 prosecutors).
- 28 lawyers' associations or law societies have been closed
- 550 lawyers have been arrested; 1,398 lawyers are facing criminal prosecution.
- At least 39 lawyers have already been sentenced to prison

I give this long list in order to underscore the scale of the transformation that is taking place in Turkey through the post-coup attempt purge. The media, civic sector, legal profession, and judiciary have been massively weakened, crippled even, in these purges. This is a generational event. These firings, arrests, and closures have largely been done on the basis of guilt by association, without due process or appropriate legal remedies.

Emergency decrees under the state of emergency also significantly changed important protections for individuals subject to investigation:

- Suspects could be held for up to 30 days without access to a lawyer. A later emergency decree reduced this length of time to 14 days.
- The right to confidential conversations with a lawyer and family members was suspended.
- The prosecution was empowered reject the defendant's choice of lawyer.
- A suspect's lawyer may have restricted access to the case file.

These and other serious derogations from due process protections have contributed to an environment in which there are increasing reports of torture and forced disappearances in detention.

In April 2017, Turkey approved in a referendum changes to the constitution that will strengthen the presidency at the expense of other branches of government, including the judiciary. The referendum, held under a state of emergency with media seized by the government, and journalists and opposition leaders in prison, was neither free nor fair. There are reasonable grounds to suspect that the government used fraud to get it barely above the 50 percent threshold.

The referendum changes increased the president's control over the judiciary by giving him power to appoint almost half (6 out of 13) of the members of the Council of Judges and Prosecutors. Others will be appointed by the parliament, which currently is under control of the president's party, the AKP. The oversight role of the Constitutional Court (*Anayasa Mahkemesi*) has been downgraded, as has that of the Council of State (*Danıştay*). Other changes in the referendum strengthened the president's powers over other branches, including through powers to appoint and dismiss ministers, to dissolve parliament, and to issue decrees with the force of law. This has turned Turkey's system of governance into a "super-presidential" system that is alien to democratic traditions.

It is within this context that we should understand the ordeal that Pastor Brunson and his family have suffered, as well as the treatment of tens of thousands of others under arrest, including people like the arrested civil society leader Osman Kavala and America's two detained foreign service nationals, Metin Topuz and Hamza Uluçay. Having eliminated due process protections and the separation of powers, the executive branch is constrained neither by the balance of powers nor by the rights of individuals.

Looking ahead

Turkey will hold three major elections in 2019: nationwide local elections, scheduled for March, and the parliamentary and presidential elections, both scheduled for November. Each of these is extremely important for President Erdoğan's goal of remaining in power and retaining or even better strengthening his control over the levers of the state. Erdoğan and his AKP no longer command the dominant big tent coalition of the 2000s that combined business, Islamists, Kurds, and liberals. The big tent has shrunk, and Erdoğan's appeal is based now more on patronage and appeals to Turkish nationalism, Islamic identity, and Eurasianism. Regardless of what the U.S. and the EU do or don't do, President Erdoğan and the AKP need anti-Western and nationalist appeals to keep his coalition together. Where the appeals fail, repression and instrumentalization of the judicial system will fill in the gaps.

For this reason, we should not expect an improvement in the rule of law in Turkey in the next two years. It is not in Erdoğan's or the AKP's interest to make the system work more fairly or more justly. Nor should we expect an improvement after the elections. If Erdoğan wins, he will continue his efforts to consolidate a patronal regime. If he loses, he will have to tighten the screws in order to maintain his grip on power, just as he did after the AKP lost its majority in parliament in the June 2015 general election. The problem of rule of law in Turkey is a durable one that we will be dealing with for a long time.

Conclusion and recommendations

1. The biggest problem with U.S. policy presently towards Turkey is that it is driven by trying to figure out what will placate Turkey, but more specifically, President Erdoğan, rather than by a clear definition of U.S. interests and values in the relationship. This has given the inaccurate impressions that the U.S. needs Erdoğan more than Erdoğan needs the U.S. **The U.S. should recognize that Erdoğ an's use of anti-Americanism and anti-Westernism is driven by a specific domestic political dynamic, and nothing the United States does will change this.**

2. Instead of starting from the position of seeking to solve the problem of anti-Western actions and rhetoric from Turkey's political leaders, **the U.S. should define clearly first for itself what its core interests and values are in its relationship with Turkey, and then articulate policies to achieve these interests, including by taking measures with Turkey to enforce those interests and values if they are threatened or violated.**

3. **I believe the U.S. has a long-term, strategic interest in Turkey being a stable state based on the rule of law, in which political and ethnic minorities enjoy fundamental rights, including the ability to participate fully in political processes.** I believe this strategic interest is of equal importance to the immediate interest of keeping Turkey in NATO. While the U.S. cannot make Turkey into such a state, this should be a key pillar of any U.S. strategic vision for the Middle East, and one that can be supported through measures taken now.

- **First, the U.S. should consider the use of additional instruments, including Global Magnitsky sanctions on Turkish officials responsible for grave human rights violations.** Congress should make use of its lawful role in forwarding such cases and requesting the State Department's official review of evidence. The compilation of such cases will play an important role in any future transition in Turkey towards a more just and inclusive regime.

- **Second, both Congress and the State Department should provide funding for human rights defenders, civil society activists, and journalists in Turkey.** Statements of support are welcome, but Congress should take the next step. Congress should create a special fund for Turkish civil society and independent media, and make a priority support for the tens of millions of Turkish citizens who see the country's future as a democratic, rule of law state.

- **Third, the United States should make clear that the following items are not up for transaction in the U.S.-Turkey relationship:**

The rule of law in the United States. Attempts to change the outcome of judicial processes in the United States with disregard for normal diplomatic and legal channels, as has occurred with the hiring of American lobbyists on behalf of Reza Zarrab and the attempt to make the extradition of Fethullah Gülen a political and not evidentiary issue, will damage the U.S.-Turkey relationship. Similarly, if Turkish officials flout U.S. law, they will face criminal prosecution. The prosecution of Reza Zarrab and Turkish officials for the flagrant violation of the sanctions regime on Iran is an important signal that violations of U.S. laws will be punished. On a lesser scale but also important is the prosecution of individuals and presidential bodyguards who assaulted protesters at Sheridan Circle in May. **The Van Hollen amendment to SFOPS reinforces this principle by underscoring that such criminal actions may affect U.S. support and cooperation with Turkey.**

American citizens and employees of the U.S. Government. The U.S. will protect its citizens accused of crimes overseas, and insist on both consular access to them and access for them to lawyers of their choosing. If it concludes the detention of an American citizen is not based on a legitimate criminal accusation, it should sanction officials responsible for their detention. **This is why the Lankford-Shaheen amendment to SFOPS is a good idea.** The U.S. should also stress that the offensive conspiracy theory put forward by prosecutors and pro-government media about former State Department official Henri Barkey will have consequences for bilateral relations, and make clear it will protect its employees, including non-Americans, from undue and illegitimate criminal prosecution. The continuing detention of two of our foreign service nationals should result in the continuation of visa restrictions and other punitive measures as needed. **Congress should also request sanctions against individual officials responsible for the illegitimate detention of U.S. employees.**

These are practical recommendations for strengthening U.S. Turkey policy, but they are not a magic bullet. We should prepare ourselves for a very rocky short-term relationship, and take the necessary measures to protect the U.S.'s core interests. The U.S.-Turkey relationship is of great consequence. It is my hope that the U.S. will stand with the many Turkish citizens working for true democracy and rule of law in Turkey, and that circumstances will one day improve to allow the bilateral relationship to return to a less tense basis.

Thank you.

MATERIAL FOR
THE RECORD

Question 1:

In recent months, Turkey has withdrawn from three "Human Dimension" meetings of the Organization for Security and Cooperation in Europe (OSCE) because of its objections to the participation of a U.S.-registered NGO it considers to be associated with the Gülen movement. Ankara is engaged in a campaign to block such NGOs from participating in other UN and OSCE events. Turkey has also withdrawn its major contributor status from the Council of Europe after the Parliamentary Assembly of the Council of Europe (PACE) awarded the Václav Havel Human Rights Prize 2017 to someone Turkey considers associated with Gülen. How is the United States responding to these actions?

Answer 1:

The State Department is concerned about recent Turkish government actions that have complicated operations at the OSCE, and by Turkey's announcement that it would withdraw its major contribution status from the Council of Europe. Civil society participation is a cornerstone of these organizations and a critical part of many events, including the OSCE's Human Dimension Implementation Meeting. We have raised this issue at high levels with the Government of Turkey, emphasizing the importance of international organizations in preserving stability and facilitating international cooperation, and encouraging Turkey to share any evidence that might help the international community respond to its concerns.

The Austrian Chairperson-in-Office of the OSCE formed a "reflection group" led by the Swiss delegation to discuss Turkey's concerns. The U.S. delegation is a part of this group, which has met several times and continues to seek a resolution.

We are also closely monitoring Turkey's recent actions in the Council of Europe and engaging allies in the organization on how its member states and the Council itself will respond. Turkey's full participation, including upholding its human rights, democracy, and rule of law commitments under the European convention and maintaining its major donor contribution, is important to the credibility and operations of the organization and of significant benefit to Turkey.

Question 2:

What human rights and rule of law-focused training or capacity building programs does the U.S. Government provide to Turkish government institutions, particularly the judiciary and law enforcement, if any?

Answer 2:

At present, the Department of State's targeted programming in Turkey prioritizes work with civil society and other diverse stakeholders in support of human rights and fundamental freedoms. These programs contribute to safeguarding rule of law, government transparency, and public awareness of government policy and practices. We would be happy to provide further details in a classified setting.

Question 3:

To the extent that Privacy Act restrictions allow you to answer, does the State Department have consular access to all U.S. citizens detained on coup-related charges in Turkey, including dual citizens? Are you satisfied with the degree of consular access? Do all of these individuals have access to legal counsel?

Answer 3:

In mid-October, after sustained U.S. Government engagement, the Government of Turkey granted the Department of State consular access to dual nationals after we permitted a senior Turkish official to meet with arrested U.S.-Turkish dual nationals in the United States. Our subsequent requests for follow-up consular access to U.S.-Turkish dual national detainees are pending with the Turkish government. We appreciate the consular access that we have received, and encourage the Turkish government to continue to allow regular consular access to U.S. citizens who also hold Turkish citizenship. Due to the requirements of the Privacy Act, we are unable to comment on access to legal counsel.

Question 4:

While Turkey is not required by the Vienna Convention on Consular Relations to provide consular access to dual US-Turkish citizens, what sort of consular access to dual US citizens does the United States receive in other NATO countries?

Answer 4:

Although not legally required to do so under international law, other NATO partners—as a courtesy—generally give us consular notification of detention and access to dual U.S. nationals detained abroad in their respective countries when requested by the U.S. citizen. Such notification and access, however, can be inconsistent when the detained individual's U.S. citizenship is unknown to the country of detention and/or the individual does not request access.

Question 5:

Has Pastor Brunson been formally charged?

Answer 5:

Pastor Brunson's arrest warrant contains five charges: membership in the armed terrorist organization "FETO," military espionage, attempt to overthrow or thwart the government of the Republic of Turkey, attempt to overthrow or thwart the Parliament of the Republic of Turkey, and attempt to overthrow the constitutional order of the Republic of Turkey. It is our understanding that the prosecutor is still preparing an indictment against Pastor

Brunson. Under Turkey's current state of emergency provisions, an individual may be held in detention for up to five years without an indictment.

Question 6:

What is the Administration's reaction to statements from President Erdoğan seeming to imply an interest in an exchange of Andrew Brunson for Fethullah Gülen?

Answer 6:

U.S. officials have clearly and at senior levels categorically rejected any linkage between the arrest of Andrew Brunson and Turkey's extradition request for Fethullah Gülen. The two situations and contexts are very different and the U.S. Government strongly objects to any effort to connect them.

Question 7:

Do you support proposed appropriations legislation for FY2018 that would require the State Department to identify and, in certain cases, possibly deny visas to senior Turkish officials linked by credible information to "wrongful prolonged detention" of U.S. citizens? Why or why not?

Answer 7:

One of the highest priorities of the Department of State is the safety and security of our citizens traveling and living abroad, particularly in cases where they have been wrongfully detained. The State Department supports the proposed appropriations legislation with a recommendation to modify the language in Section 7046(d) to mirror the waiver language in 7046(e). The restrictions target elements of the Government of Turkey that have engaged in activities against U.S. interests. Section 7046(d) targets the Presidential Guard, several members of which have been indicted in relation to the violent incidents in May 2017 at Sheridan Circle. Section 7046(e) targets yet to be identified individuals responsible for the unlawful detention of American citizens. The Department recommends replacing the certification requirement in 7046(d) with a waiver authority similar to that contained in 7046(e) to provide the Secretary of State greater flexibility to respond to changing conditions.

Question 8:

What is the Administration doing on behalf of detained U.S. consulate employees Hamza Uluçay and Metin Topuz regarding their treatment, visitation rights, due process, and possible release? Do they have access to legal counsel? Are they charged? Are the family members of any U.S. Mission locally employed staff currently detained or facing other official penalties?

Answer 8:

U.S. Government officials have raised multiple times and at the highest levels the cases of U.S. Consulate Istanbul employee Metin Topuz and U.S. Consulate Adana employee Hamza Uluçay, including with President Erdoğan, Prime Minister Binali Yildirim, and a range of other Turkish officials. We continue to do so as we seek a satisfactory outcome of these cases.

Despite initial delays, Mission Turkey engagement helped facilitate access to legal counsel for both Mr. Topuz and Mr. Uluçay. Both have been charged and Mr. Uluçay's trial is ongoing; his next hearing is scheduled for December 27. Our engagement is ongoing to ensure satisfactory treatment and visitation rights are maintained. Though the wife and daughter of a third Mission Turkey local employee were held without charges for nine days in October, they have since been released and no other Mission Turkey local staff or their family members are in detention.

Question 9:

Are there any members of the Turkish parliament who are openly sympathetic to our desire to release the U.S. citizens and consulate employees who have been unjustly detained?

Answer 9:

Some members of Turkey's opposition parties have criticized the Government of Turkey's actions against our locally employed staff. However, there has been no sustained public support from any party or any singular figure, likely in part due to fear that open association with the United States on these sensitive matters could prompt political or legal reprisals.

Question 10:

What, if anything, does the resumption of visa services mean for existing cases against local Turkish employees of the U.S. government and U.S. citizens arrested under the state of emergency? Under what conditions do you expect full visa services to resume?

Answer 10:

We implemented the suspension of non-immigrant visa services out of concern over the Government of Turkey's commitment to the safety and security of our diplomatic and consular personnel and facilities. We have subsequently received initial high-level assurances from the Government of Turkey that there are no additional local employees of our Mission in Turkey under investigation, that our local staff will not be detained or arrested for performing their official duties, and that Turkish authorities will inform the U.S. government in advance if the Government of Turkey intends to detain or arrest a member of our local staff. Based on these preliminary assurances, we determined the security posture had improved sufficiently to allow for the resumption of limited non-immigrant visa services in Turkey.

With Mr. Uluçay and Mr. Topuz still in custody, our concerns about the safety and security of our personnel and facilities remain. We will continue engaging our Turkish counterparts to seek a satisfactory resolution of these cases. Resumption of full visa services will depend on our assessment of the Government of Turkey's commitment to the safety and security of our diplomatic and consular personnel and facilities.

Question 11:

What core U.S. interests are at stake in the U.S-Turkey relationship?

Answer 11:

Turkey is a key NATO Ally and a valuable contributor to the Global Coalition to Defeat ISIS. Turkey has the second-largest military in the Alliance, a dynamic economy, a population of 80 million, and control over key energy transit pipelines and routes. Its critical position and regional clout have given Ankara significant influence on issues of core U.S. interest over the years—from Korea to the Balkans to Iraq to Afghanistan.

Turkey provides critical bases for U.S. and Coalition military forces, from which we conduct precision airstrikes against ISIS; carry out intelligence, surveillance, and reconnaissance flights; maintain combat search and rescue units; and resupply Coalition forces.

We share a growing commercial relationship, a wide array of educational and cultural exchanges, strong scientific cooperation, and a valuable foreign policy dialogue on issues ranging from Russian aggression in Crimea, to ending the war in Syria, to ensuring the territorial unity of Iraq. Turkey and the United States also maintain a strong defense trade relationship that currently supports upwards of $9 billion in defense sales.

Question 12:

What is the State Department's assessment of the information Turkey has supplied to justify the extradition of Fethullah Gülen? Where does the extradition request currently stand? What are the next steps for an extradition request?

Answer 12:

The information Turkey has provided to justify the extradition of Fethullah Gülen, reviewed by the Department of State and the Department of Justice, has not yet met the standard required for probable cause. We remain in close touch with Turkish authorities to ensure they understand the requirements for extradition under U.S. law and our bilateral extradition treaty. On November 20, 2017, Turkey provided additional materials related to its provisional arrest request for Mr. Gülen. The Department of State and the Department of Justice are in the process of reviewing these materials.

QUESTIONS FOR THE RECORD SUBMITTED BY HON. THOM TILLIS TO
CECE HEIL

Question 1:

Based on your familiarity with Andrew Brunson's case, why do you believe he was detained last year?

Answer 1:

Andrew Brunson's detention on October 7, 2016 is indeed perplexing. He had lived peacefully in Turkey for 23 years without any incident with Turkish authorities. Therefore, the only supposition one can make is that Pastor Brunson's detention was a part of the purge President Erdoğan implemented after the failed coup attempt in July, 2016, just a few months before Pastor Brunson's detention. Furthermore, the ridiculous nature of the allegations, as well as President Erdoğan's recent requests to trade Pastor Brunson, seem to support the supposition that Pastor Brunson's arrest and continued detention is purely political in nature.

Question 2:

Has Pastor Brunson been formally charged?

Answer 2:

Pastor Brunson has not been formally charged. He is being detained as a suspect, pending an investigation that has gone on for over a year. Meanwhile, his file has been sealed and there has been no access to any alleged evidence.

Question 3:

Do Turkish authorities give any explanation for the delay in beginning Andrew Brunson's trial? What court proceedings has he undergone in the past 13 months?

Answer 3:

According to the most recent court document, to which we have access, the Chief Public Prosecutor's Office is still conducting a judicial investigation, which remains at the evidence gathering stage, and Pastor Brunson is being detained as a suspect pending that investigation. The court proceedings have only consisted of detention hearings and appeals, as there have yet to be any formal charges.

Question 4:

To the extent you are familiar, what is Andrew Brunson's legal representation in Turkey? What challenges does his Turkish representation face?

Answer 4:

I stay in direct contact with Pastor Brunson's attorney in Turkey, Ismail Cem Halavurt. As there is no current legal proceeding occurring, the most that Mr. Halavurt can do is to continue to file appeals regarding Pastor Brunson's detention pending the investigation. One can only imagine the legal and political challenges of defending an innocent American pastor with a sealed file, who has been turned into a Turkish political prisoner.

Question 5:

Are you aware of any other Christian ministers who have been targeted by the Turkish Government in connection with the failed coup?

Answer 5:

Yes, according to the Association of Protestant Churches in Turkey, there were several Christian ministers from the United States and other countries who were accused of being a "threat to national security" and were denied entry or detained and deported, after the failed coup attempt in July of 2016.

Question 6:

Please describe the conditions of Andrew Brunson's detention. How often is he allowed outside of his cell?

Answer 6:

Pastor Brunson is only allowed outside of his cell once a week for his visitation time, as well as once a month for a phone call and a visit from the U.S. Embassy, should one occur.

QUESTIONS FOR THE RECORD SUBMITTED BY HON. THOM TILLIS TO
NATE SCHENKKAN

Question 1:

You describe the changes to Turkey's judiciary as a "generational event." What prolonged effects do you foresee of these changes for Turkey's governmental institutions, business climate, and society?

Answer 1:

In terms of governmental institutions, the narrow approval of the constitutional referendum of April 2017 means that Turkey is shifting to a "super-presidential" system. Under this system, which will go into full effect after the 2019 elections, the presidency's powers vis-a-vis the legislative and judicial branches of government will increase. The position of prime minister will be abolished, and the president will appoint and dismiss vice presidents and ministers, the appointment of which the parliament may not veto (in distinction from the United States, where cabinet appointments are subject to Senate confirmation). The president may issue decrees vaguely defined as "on matters related to executive power," may dismiss parliament, and may declare a state of emergency. The president will be able to appoint almost half of the Council of Judges and Prosecutors and will exercise disproportionate influence over the judiciary.

There have also been negative de facto changes to local governance in Turkey. Turkey's local governance has two levels: governors appointed by Ankara, and mayors directly elected by citizens of municipalities. Due to the large size of some of Turkey's cities, mayoralties have been among the most powerful political positions in the country; President Erdoğan built his career as mayor of Istanbul. A previous round of reforms increased the powers of mayors in order to strengthen local governance and initiate decentralization. Following the resumption of conflict in the southeast, however, the government has de facto rolled back these changes, using extraordinary powers to remove dozens of mayors, mostly from Kurdish-affiliated parties, and replace them with appointed "trustees." In addition, President Erdoğan has recently used political pressure to force out of office the most powerful mayors of his party, including those of Istanbul and Ankara. The model is similar to that of President Putin in Russia, who has restored direct elections for governors, but regularly removes governors prior to elections in order to install appointees who then will have an incumbent advantage.

The cumulative effect of the changes of the last four years is that Turkey's governmental institutions are becoming consolidated into a pyramid of influence with the president at the top—the famous "power vertical" of the Russian case. While the president, as in any system, may still face political constraints, the institutional constraints that distinguish a functioning democracy from an authoritarian system have largely been hollowed out.

In terms of the business climate, this consolidation increases political risk for investors. Politically guided expropriation and punitive tax inspections are now established tools of this government, and investors and businesses that run afoul of the government may face direct sanctions, for which they will have minimal recourse due to the absence of rule of law. More broadly, the loss of institutional independence affects Turkey's economic policy-making. The constitutional reforms give the president the power to draft the central government budget, and President Erdoğan has repeatedly attacked the Central Bank's independence in recent years. In particular, he has pressured the bank to lower interest rates, in contradiction to orthodox advice that insists on keeping rates higher to limit inflation. The downside risks of unaccountable and unprofessional fiscal and macroeconomic policies are growing with consolidation and the elimination of institutional checks on the president.

In terms of society at large, one of the most important long-term effects of the purge will be brain drain. The pressure on businesses, universities, media outlets, and civil society associations is driving some of Turkey's best human capital to leave, or causing Turkish citizens studying and working abroad to remain outside of the country.

Question 2:

What recourse do individuals who lost their jobs and shuttered organizations have to appeal these decisions? Are you aware of individuals or organizations who have managed to reverse these decisions?

Answer 2:

An extremely small number of individuals as of August 31, 2017, it was 1,852 out of 113,000 people purged, less than 2 percent—have been reinstated into public service via later emergency decrees, for reasons that remain unclear. Even for these individuals, there remains the stigma of having initially been purged, and the damage of having lost their jobs and possibly housing for what could have been several months. Similarly, a very small number of associations and media outlets have had their closures reversed under unclear reasons.

For the 98 percent of purged individuals who are not reinstated, because they were fired through being named individually in decrees issued under the state of emergency, the dismissals have the force of law and cannot be reviewed by the regular court system. Due to the large number of complaints about dismissals filed directly to the Constitutional Court, and under international pressure, the government said in January 2017 it would create a special commission to review cases. Tens of thousands of purged individuals have already applied to the commission for review, but it is unclear on what timeline the commission will review cases; it has yet to issue any decisions, and has only started receiving appeals this summer. With potentially over 100,000 appeals, it could take years for the commission to review all cases.

On the basis of the commission's formation, both the Constitutional Court and the European Court of Human Rights (ECtHR) have ruled that domestic remedies have not yet been exhausted, and therefore that they cannot hear appeals concerning the purges. Human rights defenders in Turkey have strongly objected to the ECtHR decision to consider the commission an effective domestic remedy, given that five of its seven of its members are appointed by the government, which issued the emergency decrees in the first place, and the other two are appointed by the Council of Judges and Prosecutors, which has itself been a target of the purges.

QUESTIONS FOR THE RECORD SUBMITTED BY HON. JEANNE SHAHEEN
TO JONATHAN R. COHEN

Question 1:

You were recently in Turkey to discuss the aftermath of the U.S.'s decision to not process visas until the Turks assured the safety of Embassy officials from arrest and shared more information on potential security threats. How did these conversations go? It is our understanding that in the period that the United State stopped processing non-resident visas for Turks, Turkey made some headway on other issues, which we don't have to detail in an open setting. Do you feel this signals the need for a new approach to Turkey?

Answer 1:

My October visit to Ankara resulted in progress that allowed for the November resumption of limited non-immigrant visa services, which were suspended due to security concerns. My discussions with Turkish officials led to assurances from the Government of Turkey that there are no additional local employees of our Mission in Turkey under investigation, that our local staff will not be detained or arrested for performing their official duties, and that Turkish authorities will inform the U.S. government in advance if the Government of Turkey intends to detain or arrest a member of our local staff. Based on these preliminary assurances, we determined the security posture had improved sufficiently to allow for the resumption of limited visa services in Turkey.

However, Mr. Uluçay and Mr. Topuz remain in custody and we continue to work tirelessly to secure a satisfactory resolution of these cases.

Our relationship with Turkey has always been complex. Despite current strains in the relationship, Turkey is a NATO Ally and valued partner. We will continue to cooperate with Turkey in areas where we share common goals and concerns and we will continue engaging Turkey's leadership in areas where we have disagreements.

Question 2:

Fifty percent of Turkey's population spoke out against Erdoğan centralization of power through the April 2017 referendum. How is the U.S. government engaging with these Turks and building bridges to those who are not necessarily in the Turkish government or security structures? What is the full U.S. contribution to developing civil society in Turkey (please breakdown according to account/program)? I appreciate that the funding was restored, but could you explain why the decision was made earlier this year to eliminate the minimal amount of funding that the U.S. devotes to help bolster Turkish civil society? This is concerning particularly since President Erdoğan is targeting and jailing prominent leaders in Turkey's civil society.

Answer 2:

The quality of Turkey's democracy, in which civil society plays a vital role, matters deeply to the United States. We regularly engage Turkey's leadership about our concerns over the government's targeting of civil society groups and leaders. We also use a broad range of traditional State Department Public Diplomacy and other tools and programs promoting civil society and democracy in Turkey. The Mission Turkey Public Diplomacy Section administers an active small grants program, providing grants to Turkish civil society organizations that support issues such as freedom of expression, countering violent extremism, understanding of democratic values and rule of law, entrepreneurship, women's rights, and STEM education. Grants have supported visits from U.S. experts, extracurricular activities for high school and university students, film festivals, cultural programs, and a host of other programs. Although these grants are relatively small in dollar value, they provide much needed support to strengthen Turkey's civil society and underscore U.S. commitment to upholding democratic values in Turkey.

Through engagements with Turkey's government and other tools, the Department of State has also worked to enhance and protect fundamental freedoms, including: supporting the human rights of particularly threatened or at-risk communities; freedom of speech and the media; promoting transparency and accountability; and enhancing legal frameworks to protect human rights. The Department would be pleased to provide further details in a classified setting.

Question 3:

Nate Schenkkan testified to the need for U.S. assistance to Turkish civil society. Since Turkey does not have a USAID mission, what is the best way to administer such assistance? Can there be parallels found in the way the U.S. administers assistance to civil society groups in other areas without a USAID mission that are also hostile to the U.S., like Russia? Which civil society groups are in the most need? Is the EU providing assistance to Turkish civil society?

Answer 3:

The Department of State implements programs worldwide focused on advancing democracy and human rights priorities, including breaking barriers that limit access to free and credible information, combatting threats against journalists, promoting freedom of religion and conscience, and addressing the shrinking space for civil society as a means to promote long-term stability. The European Union also provides civil society assistance in Turkey.

The Department's programs operate in closed and closing environments around the world, including in some of the most restrictive and hostile operating environments. We work closely with our implementing partners to continually evaluate and adjust programmatic approaches and operating procedures, and we apply lessons-learned from our experiences in other countries. All of our programs require risk mitigation strategies and contingency plans to ensure both safety of our participants and ability to adapt to worsening situations.

The Department would be pleased to provide further details in a classified setting regarding lessons learned from implementing programs in other non-USAID presence countries, and how our programs could assist civil society and help to address human rights concerns in Turkey.

Question 4:

Given the mass arrests in Turkey, do you feel that Turkish-Americans who may have been critical of the Turkish government should visit Turkey at this time? Is it safe for those who have been public about their criticisms? When do you think these Turkish-Americans should know that their safety may be in jeopardy? Do travel warnings to Turkey reflect the risks to Turkish-Americans?

Answer 4:

The most recent Turkey travel warning, issued on September 28, 2017, recommends that all U.S. citizens carefully consider the need to travel to Turkey at this time. The travel warning notes that under the state of emergency, security forces have expanded powers, including the authority to detain any person at any time. It also notes that the Turkish government has at times restricted political gatherings, scrutinized non-governmental organizations, restricted internet access, and blocked media content. The travel warning informs Turkish Americans that consular access to detained U.S. citizens who hold Turkish nationality may be denied and that Turkish authorities have legally banned some U.S. citizens, most of whom are dual U.S.-Turkish nationals, from departing Turkey.

LETTER FROM KUBRA GÖLGE TO CONGRESS

November 15, 2017

Dear Congressmen:

My husband, Serkan Gölge, and I and our two small children are dual U.S.-Turkish citizens. Until my husband's arrest last year, we were residents of Houston, Texas, where my husband had been working as a senior research scientist at the NASA Johnson Space Center. In July 2016, while we were visiting Serkan's family for a few days in Turkey, he was suddenly taken into custody as we were packing to return home to Houston. Like hundreds of others in Turkey, he has been charged with membership in the movement founded by Islamic cleric Fethullah Gü len. Because President Erdoğan has accused Mr. Gülen of ordering followers of his movement to carry out the attempted coup last year, the Gülen movement is now considered a terrorist organization. Serkan's trial began in April 2017, and his fifth hearing is scheduled for this Friday.

There is no credible evidence to support the charges against my husband. Some law enforcement officers claim that possession of a U.S. $1 bill can indicate membership in the Gülen movement. I do not understand why a U.S. citizen having a $1 can be considered criminal. I am very afraid that my husband is not receiving a fair trial. There is an atmosphere of fear in Turkey. Lawyers who defend people charged with connections to Gü len risk losing their jobs, as do the judges hearing these cases. Serkan has been imprisoned for more than 15 months—much of that time in solitary confinement—and his health is deteriorating. He has high blood pressure and kidney stones. This situation is unbearable for me and my children. We worry about Serkan's poor health. Although I am not accused of any wrongdoing, the police have told me that I am not allowed to leave Turkey. My children are only seven and two years old, and I am afraid that I won't be able to protect them if they or I are threatened by the authorities. We simply want to go home and feel safe again.

I respectfully ask for you to look into our untenable situation and help us in any way that you can. Thank you for your kind attention to this important human rights matter.

Sincerely,

Kubra Gölge

STATEMENT ON THE STATUS OF ACADEMICS AND SCIENTISTS IN TURKEY FROM THE COMMITTEE OF CONCERNED SCIENTISTS, NOVEMBER 15, 2017

HISTORY:

Good morning distinguished members, Congressmen and women, and guests. The Committee of Concerned Scientists ("CCS"), has been working with scientists and academics in Turkey for a very long time. Since January 2016 requests for our assistance have increased dramatically from this country. Problems for this population, from Turkey, have escalated as they have been the target of the Erdoğan government's recriminations for the most recent coup attempt.

The Committee of Concerned Scientists has been advocating for the human rights of scientists, physicians, engineers and academics since February 1974. Prior to that, many of our members were actively involved with the Russian Refusnik movement, which assisted scientists in communist countries get materials and information they needed; as well as helping them to get their work out of their respective countries and made available to the scientific world-at-large. Additionally, several of our Board members are Nobel Laureates. Currently, CCS works with scientists, academics, physicians and engineers whose human rights have been violated. At this point in time, Turkey is well on its way to making it to the top of the list of countries that are involved in human rights violations.

The current actions of the government of Turkey, in its sweeping purge of dissent, both real and imagined, is crippling the credibility and integrity of Turkey's academic and scientific institutions, and doing real damage to the Turkish economy and the Turkish state. The May 2017 assault by bodyguards of President Recep Tayyip Erdoğan on peaceful protestors in Washington, D.C., demonstrates how Turkish repression has the potential to spill across borders, and the detention of scores of Turkish scholars who are either resident in, or citizens of, European countries or the United States demonstrates how Turkey's continuing attack on academia is a significant threat to scholarship throughout the OSCE region.

The Commission on Security and Cooperation in Europe (U.S. Helsinki Commission) is uniquely positioned to make a difference, and we urge the Commission to make it a top priority to confront this challenge.

There was evidence of civil unrest in Turkey in January of 2016, when a Peace Petition was published accusing the Erdoğan government of carrying out heavy-handed operations against Turkey's Kurdish population. It was signed by more than 1,000 academics. At that time, the existence of such a petition upset Erdoğan and the ruling AKP Party. The government began taking retribution against the academics who signed the petition. Hundreds of academics who signed the petition were either terminated from their positions at universities, or were detained when police raided their homes and/or offices.

Shortly thereafter, an attempted coup took place on July 15, 2016. Since that time the government has mounted a widespread purge in the name of security. On the night of the coup attempt, 234 persons were killed and more than 2,000 were injured. Erdoğan was away from the seat of government at that time but was informed, and mounted a defense, ultimately thwarting the coup attempt.

The government then declared a state of emergency, suspended the rule of law (which continues to this day—over a year later) and blamed the coup on Fethullah Gü len, who earlier had been Erdoğan's ally. The relationship has deteriorated into an extremely contentious one, causing Gülen to retreat from Turkey and live in exile in the United States. (Gülen continues to deny any involvement in this coup attempt.) It appears that the academics and scientists who signed the Peace Petition back in January have been lumped into the class of those considered against the state, and therefore, "terrorists" or supporters of terrorists.

As of August 2017, 50,000 people have been arrested, and 150,000 have lost their jobs or been suspended. Of those, 7,500 are academics and college administrators, with 60,000 students being displaced. Hundreds have been arrested and jailed, awaiting outcomes of lengthy investigations and trials. Many have been charged and released while awaiting trial. Under these circumstances, those released have had to relinquish their passports, making it impossible for them to leave the country.

To add to their problems, when they apply for new jobs employers are notified that they were terminated by decree, so nobody is willing to hire them. In addition, they are banned from civil service positions. Supporting themselves and their families has become difficult to impossible. The Executive Director of Scholars at Risk, Robert Quinn, has noted that these actions against higher education institutions, scholars, staff and students strongly suggest retaliation for the non-violent exercise of academic freedom, freedom of expression and freedom of association. This is especially true of actions against individuals based solely on their public endorsement of the Academics for Peace petition or their alleged affinity for the so-called Gulenist movement.

PROBLEMS FOR ACADEMICS/SCIENTISTS:

- Loss of jobs
- Loss of tenure
- Loss of freedom
- Criminal charges
- Inability to Pursue Studies
- Inability to Provide for Self/Family
- Inability to Leave Country—Jailed within country borders or passport seized
- Inability to Enter Country
- Missing family events (weddings, graduations, births, funerals, etc.)

- Long periods of detention
- Long periods awaiting trials
- Labeled as traitors and terrorists
- Names end up on decree lists, virtually ending life as once lived
- Growing number of classes and courses without instructors

Prominent Cases of Scientists/Academics Impacted:

Istar Gozaydin:

A professor of Sociology from Gediz University and a founder of Turkey's branch of the Helsinki Citizens' Assembly, Istar Gozaydin was detained and arrested in December 2016 on vague terrorism-related charges. She started a hunger strike, and one hundred days after her detention she was released, but barred from traveling, and she is expected to return to court to face charges of "being a member of a terrorist organization."

Muzzafer Kaya, Esra Mungan and Kivanc Ersoy:

The government of Turkey was cracking down on dissent, human rights and academic freedom, well before the July 2016 coup attempt. A Peace Petition, signed by over 1,000 academics and read out at a press conference in January 2016, drew a swift and brutal response from the government of Turkey, with 27 academics suspended and at least 30 dismissed from their jobs. All the signers of the Peace Petition were placed under investigation, perversely, for crimes of "terrorism". By March 2016, three academics—Muzzafer Kaya (social work), Esra Mungan (psychology), and Kivanc Ersoy (mathematics)—had been arrested for "making terrorist propaganda". They have had been arrested for "making terrorist propaganda". They have had five hearings and are awaiting a sixth in December while the court considers a request from the prosecutor in the case to change to charges to "insulting the Turkish nation".

Serkan Gölge:

A Turkish-American scientist who works for NASA, Serkan Gölge has been detained since July 2016 and placed in solitary confinement after an estranged family member reported him for spying. Has since been charged with being a supporter of Gülen.

Nuriye Gülmen and Semih Özakça:

After the July 2016 coup attempt, the crackdown on academia intensified. Like thousands of other scholars and academic professionals, professor of literature Gülmen and an elementary school teacher Özakça were summarily dismissed from their jobs in November 2016, without explanation. Exercising their right to protest, they began a hunger strike in March 2017, and in May they were detained on absurd charges of "membership in a terrorist organization" and "propaganda for a terrorist organization". Özakça was ordered released on October 20 (though required to wear an electronic monitor), but Gülmen remains imprisoned. On November 8, their lawyer, who is also the president of the Progressive Lawyers' Association (Ç HD), Selçuk Kozağ açli, was also detained, and on Monday was remanded to prison, also charged with membership in a terrorist organization. Their case illustrates the uncompromising intolerance of dissent and complete disdain for human rights that has overtaken the Turkish government. Its ongoing purge has destroyed tens of thousands of promising academic careers.

Ismail Kul:

Many scholars have been arrested by the government of Turkey because of perceived connections to Fethullah Gü len, the U.S. based expat alleged by the Turkish government to bear responsibility for the July 2016 coup attempt. Some Turkish-American academics have been detained and are clearly being held as bargaining chips in the Turkish government's quest to have Gülen extradited back to Turkey. Ismail Kul, a U.S.-based chemistry professor at Widener University in Delaware, was arrested in August 2016, and has been in detention ever since, because he had met Fethullah Gülen. This, despite the fact that it was Ahmet Aydin, a prominent member of the current ruling Justice and Development Party (AKP) of Turkey who had introduced Professor Kul to Gülen. This cynical effort to detain academics and scholars on such flimsy pretexts, all for the purpose of facilitating a trade for Gülen, is cruel and profoundly unjust, and it is destroying innocent lives.

Ahmet Turan Özcerit:

An Associate professor at Sakarya University's Faculty of Computer and Information Science, Ahmet Turan Özcerit was arrested and detained for 13 months. He was eventually release after being diagnosed with liver and intestinal cancer.

There are just stories, after stories, after stories of professors and scientists who have lost their jobs, are being detained, and have been arrested and charged as members of "terrorist" organizations.

Action for the Helsinki Commission, Congresspersons, Citizens

The ongoing systematic and ruthless degrading of Turkey's academic and scientific institutions is a profound tragedy, not just for Turkey, but for the whole OSCE region, and indeed the world. It is vital that action be taken to reverse this trend and restore Turkey to its rightful place as an indispensable player on the global scientific and academic stage. We urge the U.S. Helsinki Commission to make the current assault of science, scholarship, and basic human rights in Turkey a top priority.

We urge the Commission to develop and promote policies that will protect the rights of Turkish scientists and scholars to travel within the OSCE region, and to proactively work to ensure that academics at risk in Turkey are able to relocate safely to other OSCE countries where they can continue their scholarly pursuits.

We urge the Commission to actively engage all OSCE governments to demand that the government of Turkey respect the human rights of scholars and scientists, including the rights to freedom of speech, assembly, and belief; as well as the rights to travel and enjoy basic academic freedoms. The government of Turkey must also be called upon in the strongest possible terms to end the use of torture, arbitrary detention, and unfair trials.

We urge the Commission to work with OSCE governments to bring about a just resolution in the cases of the scholars mentioned above, as well as the thousands of other Turkish scholars and scientists who have been unjustly imprisoned or wrongfully dismissed from their academic institutions.

Turkey

	2016	2017
Internet Freedom Status	Not Free	Not Free
Obstacles to Access (0-25)	13	13
Limits on Content (0-35)	21	23
Violations of User Rights (0-40)	27	30
TOTAL* (0-100)	61	66

* 0=most free, 100=least free

Population:	79.5 million
Internet Penetration 2016 (ITU):	58.4 percent
Social Media/ICT Apps Blocked:	Yes
Political/Social Content Blocked:	Yes
Bloggers/ICT Users Arrested:	Yes
Press Freedom 2017 Status:	Not Free

Key Developments: June 2016 – May 2017

- After protests erupted over the removal from office f 28 mayors in the Kurdish-majority southeast, authorities restricted internet access for approximately 12 million residents in the region (see **Restrictions on Connectivity**).

- Access to Twitter, Facebook, and YouTube was repeatedly disrupted in the aftermath of terrorist attacks, while Wikipedia was permanently blocked over articles on Turkey's involvement in the Syrian civil war (see **Blocking and Filtering**).

- Turkey accounted for 65 percent of all content that was locally restricted by Twitter during the coverage period, as the government cracked down on independent reporting (see **Content Removal**).

- The hacktivist group RedHack leaked over 57,000 emails from Berat Albayrak, son-in-law of President Recep Tayyip Erdoğan, revealing the extent of a government campaign to manipulate social media and smear prominent opposition figu es (see **Media, Diversity, and Content Manipulation** and **Technical Attacks**).

- The government has implemented an arbitrary and disproportionate purge of state officials, eachers, journalists, and others, dismissing or arresting them for alleged ties to a July 2016 coup attempt based on flimsy ci cumstantial evidence, including communication apps allegedly found on their phones, attendance at a digital security training in Istanbul, and tweets that criticized the government (see **Prosecutions and Detentions for Online Activities**).

Introduction

Internet freedom sharply declined in Turkey in 2017 due to the repeated suspension of telecommunications networks and social media access, as well as sweeping arrests for political speech online.

During the coverage period, Turkey suffered more than a dozen terrorist attacks, an economic and monetary crisis, and a failed coup on July 15, 2016, in which a rogue faction of the Turkish military attempted to overthrow the government. Internet connections were throttled, and major social media platforms were blocked. Loyalist forces later reestablished internet service, and President Erdoğan addressed the nation through a FaceTime video call made to a television news anchor on CNN Türk, urging citizens to take to the streets in a show of support for the government. Order was eventually restored, but not before some 300 people were killed in clashes between pro- and anticoup forces. Government officials publicly blamed exiled Islamic p eacher Fethullah Gülen for instigating the coup. A state of emergency was declared on July 20, allowing the Council of Ministers (cabinet), chaired by President Erdoğan, to issue decrees without parliamentary or judicial oversight.

Since then, the government has implemented a massive purge in which more than 60,000 citizens have been arrested for alleged connections to Gülen or other banned groups, while over 140,000 have been suspended or dismissed from their jobs.[1] In addition, at least 5 news agencies, 62 newspapers, 16 television channels, 19 periodicals, 29 publishing houses, and 24 radio stations have been forcibly closed down by decree.[2] Despite the ongoing state of emergency, authorities went ahead with a referendum to grant greater power to the president and abolish the office f prime minister.[3] The constitutional amendments, which would take effect in 2019, passed with 51.4 percent of the vote in April 2017, though the process was criticized by independent monitors from the Organization for Security and Co-operation in Europe. Erdoğan, who was elected as prime minister in 2003 and then became president in 2014, could theoretically remain in power until 2029 due to a clause that reset term limits.[4]

The government has repeatedly suspended access to Facebook, Twitter, YouTube, and WhatsApp on national security grounds, while Wikipedia has been permanently blocked due to articles related to Turkey's role in the Syrian civil war. Popular services offering virtual private networks (VPNs) and the Tor anonymity network have been blocked to prevent users from accessing censored content. At the same time, ongoing tensions between the Kurdish minority and the central government resulted in the arrest of parliamentarians, mayors, and officials f om the pro-Kurdish People's Democratic Party (HDP), which the government accused of ties to the Kurdistan Workers' Party (PKK), a Kurdish militant group that is classified as a errorist organization by Turkey, the United States, and a number of other governments. A 23-year-old fine a ts student was sentenced to more than four years in prison after posting political tweets that were deemed to promote terrorist propaganda and insultthe president. The government has used similar charges to detain scores of journalists, political activists, and ordinary citizens for little more than criticizing the ruling Justice and Development Party (AKP), often using their social media posts as evidence in court. Turkish users must also

---

1   See Turkey Purge at https://turkeypurge.com/
2   CHP, "Sarihan: Gece Yarisi Kararnameleri ile Gelen Karanlik: Bu Bir Kiyimdir! Kiyima Hayir!," February 9, 2017, https://www.chp.org.tr/Haberler/4/sarihan-gece-yarisi-kararnameleri-ile-gelen-karanlik-bu-bir-kiyimdir-kiyima-hayir-53283.aspx
3   "Questions and Answers: Turkey's Constitutional Referendum," Human Rights Watch, April 4, 2017, https://www.hrw.org/news/2017/04/04/questions-and-answers-turkeys-constitutional-referendum
4   James Masters and Kara Fox, "International monitors deliver scathing verdict on Turkish referendum," CNN, April 18, 2017, http://www.cnn.com/2017/04/17/europe/turkey-referendum-results-Erdoğan/index.html

contend with intrusive government surveillance and the proven use of sophisticated malware tools by law enforcement agencies. In a country where the government reportedly listed social media as one of the main threats to national security,[5] internet freedom remains on a starkly negative trajectory.

Obstacles to Access

The most significant obstacle to internet access in Turkey remains the practice of shutting down telecommunications networks during security operations, mainly in the southeastern part of the country. Internet penetration continues to grow, particularly through mobile broadband, as three companies have begun to offer "4.5G" services.

Availability and Ease of Access

Key Access Indicators		
Internet penetration (ITU)[a]	2016	58.4%
	2015	53.7%
	2011	43.1%
Mobile penetration (ITU)[b]	2016	97%
	2015	96%
	2011	89%
Average connection speeds (Akamai)[c]	2017(Q1)	7.6 Mbps
	2016(Q1)	7.2 Mbps

[a] International Telecommunication Union, "Percentage of Individuals Using the Internet, 2000-2016," http://bit.ly/1cbbxY.
[b] International Telecommunication Union, "Mobile-Cellular Telephone Subscriptions, 2000-2016," http://bit.ly/1cbbxY.
[c] Akamai, "State of the Internet - Connectivity Report, Q1 2017," https://goo.gl/TQH7L7.

Internet penetration has continued to increase over the last few years. According to the International Telecommunication Union, it stood at 58.35 percent at the end of 2016, up from 43.07 percent fi e years earlier.[6] There were 53.5 million mobile broadband subscribers as of the fi st quarter of 2017, while the number of fi ed broadband subscribers stood at 772,325.[7] Regular mobile subscriptions reached 75.7 million, representing a penetration rate of over 107 percent.

According to the results of the Turkish Statistical Institute's Household Usage of Information Technologies Survey, the share of households with internet access has risen to 76 percent.[8] For individuals aged 16–74, computer usage stood at 95.9 percent, and internet usage was 93.7 percent.

---

5   The National Security Council allegedly listed social media as one of the main threats to Turkey's national security, along with protests and civil disobedience; parallel state structures; communication security; cyber security; organizations exploiting religion, such as the Islamic State militant group; and ethnic-based terrorist groups, such as the Kurdistan Workers' Party (PKK). "National Security Council under Erdoğan updates top secret national security 'book,'" *Hurriyet Daily News*, April 30, 2015, http://bit.ly/1UV8cCM

6   International Telecommunication Union, "Statistics," 2016, http://www.itu.int/en/ITU-D/Statistics/Pages/stat/default.aspx

7   Information and Communication Technologies Authority, "Electronic Communications Market in Turkey – Market Data (2017 Q1)," https://www.btk.gov.tr/File/?path=ROOT%2f1%2fDocuments%2fPages%2fMarket_Data%2f2017_Q1_Eng.pdf

8   Turkiye Istatistik Kurumu, "Household Usage of Information Technologies Survey of Turkish Statistical Institute, 2015," [in Turkish] August 18, 2015, accessed October 13, 2016, http://www.tuik.gov.tr/PreTablo.do?alt_id=1028

TURKEY

Prices remain high in comparison with the minimum wage. Turkey ranked 70th on the global ICT Development Index (IDI) for 2016, one spot down from the previous year.[9]

Restrictions on Connectivity

Restrictions on connectivity are frequent, particularly in the restive southeastern region, where ethnic Kurds form a majority. On September 11, 2016, landline, mobile phone, and internet services were shut down in 10 cities for six hours, affecting some 12 million residents. The shutdown related to the forced removal of 28 Kurdish mayors from their posts.[10] One month later, the government suspended mobile and fi ed-line internet service in 11 cities for several days, leaving 6 million citizens offline. ey public services, such as banks and payment mechanisms, were reportedly unavailable. The shutdown coincided with mass protests prompted by the detention of local Kurdish politicians, including the two co-mayors of Diyarbakır, and was apparently intended to delay or inhibit coverage of the police response. Reporters were forced to travel to nearby cities in order to upload and share footage of police beating protesters.[11] Shutdowns have often been imposed during military operations in the region. Connectivity is also affected by poor telecommunications infrastructure and electricity blackouts.

Turkey's internet backbone is run by TTNET, a subsidiary of Türk Telekom that is also the largest internet service provider (ISP) in the country. Türk Telekom, which is partly state owned, has 234,176 km of fibe -optic infrastructure, with around half of it serving as backbone infrastructure. Other operators have a combined total of 63,444 km of fiber length.[12]

There are three internet exchange points (IXPs) owned by private companies: IST-IX, established by Terramark in 2009; TNAP, established by seven leading ISPs in 2013; and DEC-IX, a German company that established its operation in Istanbul as "a neutral interconnection and peering point for internet service providers from Turkey, Iran, the Caucasus region and the Middle East."[13]

ICT Market

There were 446 operators providing information and communications technology (ICT) services in the Turkish market in the fi st quarter of 2017.[14] There are around 359 ISPs, though the majority act as resellers for Türk Telekom. TTNET, founded in 2006 by Türk Telekom, is the dominant player, with a market share of more than 70 percent.[15]

Turkcell is the leading mobile phone provider, with 44.1 percent of the market, followed by Vodafone

9   International Telecommunication Union, *ICT Development Index 2016*, http://www.itu.int/net4/ITU-D/idi/2016/

10   Bilge Yesil and Efe Kerem Sozeri, "Turkey's Internet Policy after the Coup Attempt," June 28, 2016, http://globalnetpolicy. org/wp-content/uploads/2017/02/Turkey1_v6-1.pdf

11   The 11 cities were Diyarbakır, Mardin, Batman, Siirt, Van, Elazığ, Tunceli, Gaziantep, Şanlıurfa, Kilis and Adıyaman. Turkey Blocks, "New internet shutdown in Turkey's Southeast: 8% of country now offline amidst Diyar akir unrest," October 27, 2016, https://turkeyblocks.org/2016/10/27/new-internet-shutdown-turkey-southeast-offline-diyar_akir-unrest/

12   Information and Communication Technologies Authority, "Electronic Communications Market in Turkey – Market Data (2017 Q1)," https://www.btk.gov.tr/File/?path=ROOT%2f1%2fDocuments%2fPages%2fMarket_Data%2f2017_Q1_Eng.pdf

13   "DEC-IX Istanbul," accessed February 20, 2015, https://www.de-cix.net/products-services/de-cix-istanbul/

14   Information and Communication Technologies Authority, "Electronic Communications Market in Turkey – Market Data (2017 Q1)," https://www.btk.gov.tr/File/?path=ROOT%2f1%2fDocuments%2fPages%2fMarket_Data%2f2017_Q1_Eng.pdf

15   Information and Communication Technologies Authority, "Electronic Communications Market in Turkey – Market Data (2016 Q1)," accessed October 10, 2016, slide 34, http://www.btk.gov.tr/ File/?path=ROOT%2f1%2fDocuments%2fPages%2fMarket_Data%2f2016-Q1-En.pdf

and Avea (which currently operates under the brand Türk Telekom).[16] An auction of 4G frequency bands was held in August 2015, and by April 2016, all three of these companies had started offering "4.5G" technology to mobile subscribers.[17]

Though all legal entities are allowed to operate an ISP, there are some requirements to apply for authorization, pertaining to issues like the company's legal status, its scope of activity, and its shareholders' qualifications. Info mal obstacles may also prevent newly founded companies without political ties or economic clout from entering the market. ISPs are required by law to submit an application for an "activity certifica e" to the Information and Communication Technologies Authority (BTK) before they can offer services. Internet cafés are subject to regulation as well. Those operating without an activity certifica e from a local municipality may face fines f TRY 3,000 to 15,000 (US$800 to US$4,000). Mobile phone service providers are subject to licensing through the BTK. Moreover, the BTK has the authority to request written notifications f om ISPs. In December 2016, BTK asked all ISPs to submit weekly progress reports on the status of new restrictions on virtual private networks (VPNs).[18]

Regulatory Bodies

Policymaking, regulation, and operation functions are separated under the basic laws of the telecommunications sector. The Ministry of Transportation, Maritime Affairs, and Communications is responsible for policymaking, while the BTK is in charge of regulation.[19]

The BTK has its own dedicated budget, but its board members are government appointees and its decision-making process is not transparent. Nonetheless, there have been no reported instances of certifica es or licenses being denied. After the 2016 coup attempt, the Telecommunication and Communication Presidency (TİB), which implemented the country's website blocking law, was shut down under an emergency decree. All of its responsibilities were transferred to the BTK.[20] The TİB—described by President Erdoğan as "among the places that has all the dirt"—was closed due to suspicions that it was used by Gülenists as a "headquarters for illegal wiretapping."[21]

The Computer Center of Middle East Technical University has been responsible for managing domain names since 1991. The BTK oversees and establishes the domain-name operation policy and its bylaws. Unlike in many other countries, individuals in Turkey are not permitted to register and own domain names ending with the country extension .tr, such as .com.tr and .org.tr, unless they own a trademark, company, or civil society organization with the same name as the requested domain.

16   Information and Communication Technologies Authority, "Electronic Communications Market in Turkey – Market Data (2017 Q1)," https://www.btk.gov.tr/File/?path=ROOT%2f1%2fDocuments%2fPages%2fMarket_Data%2f2017_Q1_Eng.pdf

17   Tuley Karadeniz, "Turkey's 4G tender outstrips predictions with bids for 4.5 billion," Reuters, August 26, 2015, http://www.reuters.com/article/2015/08/26/us-turkey-telecoms-idUSKCN0QV1XI20150826

18   Fusun S. Nebil, "BTK'nın VPN Engelleme Israrı Devam Ediyor," Turk-Internet, December 5, 2016, http://www.turk-internet.com/portal/yazigoster.php?yaziid=54731

19   Information and Communication Technologies Authority, "Establishment," accessed October 11, 2015, http://bit.ly/1QsTRoE

20   "Turkey shuts down telecommunication body amid post-coup attempt measures," Hurriyet Daily News, August 15, 2016, http://www.hurriyetdailynews.com/turkey-shuts-down-telecommunication-body-amid-post-coup-attempt-measures.aspx?pageID=238&nID=102936&NewsCatID=338

21   "Turkey shuts down telecommunication body amid post-coup attempt measures," Hurriyet Daily News, August 15, 2016, http://www.hurriyetdailynews.com/turkey-shuts-down-telecommunication-body-amid-post-coup-attempt-measures.aspx?pageID=238&nID=102936&NewsCatID=338

Limits on Content

Limits on content continued to increase in Turkey over the past year. In response to a series of deadly terrorist attacks and the coup attempt, the government repeatedly blocked or throttled social media platforms as well as instant messaging services in a bid to halt the dissemination of images and other information pertaining to the events. In addition, scores of news sites and Twitter accounts were blocked or removed, particularly those covering the government's conflict with Kurdish militants. Journalists, scholars, and public figures who are critical of the government faced coordinated harassment by progovernment trolls on Twitter.

Blocking and Filtering

Blocking continues to expand steadily in Turkey. Engelliweb, a website that tracked total blocking figu es, found that more than 114,000 websites were inaccessible as of November 2016, up from about 40,000 in 2013. More recent figu es are unavailable, as the website and its social media accounts have been closed down without explanation. Over 90 percent of websites were blocked due to "obscenity," which includes any site with certain sexual keywords in the domain, resulting in the collateral blocking of several websites related to the LGBT (lesbian, gay, bisexual, and transgender) community.[22] Websites are also blocked if they are deemed defamatory to Islam, including websites that promote atheism.[23] However, the most recent uptick in censored content during the coverage period relates to news sites, particularly those whose editorial policies conflict with the populist media narrative of the government.

The BTK and Turkish courts blocked access to at least 17 news sites during the coverage period, including Medyascope, *Yarına Bakış, Yeni Hayat Gazetesi,* Can Erzincan TV, *Gazeteport, Haberdar,*[24] *Karşı Gazete,* dokuz8haber, and the relaunched website of the left-leaning news outlet Jiyan, Jiyan. us.[25] A judge closed the pro-Kurdish daily *Ozgur Gundem* and news agency DİHA due to alleged "terrorist organisation propaganda,"[26] and the website and social media accounts of İMC TV were blocked after its license was revoked by decree.[27] A news website operated by prominent journalist Can Dundar, Ozguruz.org, was blocked before it had even published any news.[28]

Facebook, Twitter, YouTube, and other services were briefly bloc ed or throttled on multiple occasions during the coverage period:

---

22   Bilge Yesil and Efe Kerem Sozeri, "Turkey's Internet Policy after the Coup Attempt," June 28, 2016, http://globalnetpolicy. org/wp-content/uploads/2017/02/Turkey1_v6-1.pdf

23   Golbasi Criminal Court of Peace Decision No 2015/191 D.Is, dated February 27 2015; Efe Kerem Sözeri, "Turkey quietly escalating online censorship of atheism," *The Daily Dot,* March 4, 2015, http://bit.ly/1M9kZpa

24   "Arrested for "praising the coup"?," IFEX, July 25, 2016, https://www.ifex.org/turkey/2016/07/25/coup_aftermath/

25   Efe Kerem Sozeri, "Turkey declares war on ISIS, censors Kurdish news instead", 2 August, 2015, https://medium.com/@ efekerem/turkey-declares-war-on-isis-censors-kurdish-news-instead-3f30a9e5264f#.b5hmjmor2

26   Elif Akgul, "Özgür Gündem Newspaper Shut Down," BIANet, August 16, 2016, http://bianet.org/english/media/177853-ozgur-gundem-newspaper-shut-down

27   "Turkey closes 20 TV and radio stations in post-coup clampdown," The Guardian, September 30, 2016, https://www. theguardian.com/world/2016/sep/30/turkey-closes-20-tv-and-radio-stations-post-coup-clampdown

28   "Ozguruz.org Blocked Before Site Could Publish Any News," BIANet, January 27, 2017, http://bianet.org/english/ media/183060-ozguruz-org-blocked-before-site-could-publish-any-news

---

- Facebook and Twitter were throttled for two hours after a terrorist attack on Istanbul Ataturk Airport killed 38 people on June 28, 2016.[29]

- Twitter, Facebook, and YouTube were blocked between 11 p.m. and 12 a.m. local time on the day of the coup attempt, July 15, 2016. The government subsequently ordered ISPs to lift the ban on social media sites to help spread President Erdoğan's call on citizens to defend the country.[30]

- On August 20, 2016, a suicide bomber targeted a Kurdish wedding in Gaziantep, killing 57 people and wounding 60 others. After the attack, Turkey's Radio and Television Supreme Council (RTÜK) issued a media ban, resulting in the blocking of Facebook, Twitter, and YouTube for six hours.[31]

- On August 25, 2016, Twitter, Facebook, and YouTube were inaccessible for more than seven hours.[32] Observers could not definiti ely point to one incident to explain the outage.

- Following the arrest of 11 HDP parliamentarians on November 4, 2016, Twitter, Facebook, YouTube, and WhatsApp were throttled. Prime Minister Binali Yıldırım justified the blocking as a " emporary security measure."[33]

- On December 19, 2016, Facebook, Twitter, YouTube, and WhatsApp were blocked for over 10 hours following the assassination of Russian ambassador Andrey Karlov.[34] Later, a judge ordered the blocking of more than 100 URLs related to the assassination,[35] including the news site of the Dutch Broadcast Foundation (NOS).[36]

- After the release of footage of the immolation of two Turkish soldiers by Islamic State (IS) militants on December 22, 2016, Twitter, Facebook, YouTube,[37] and the Turkish social media site Ekşi Sözlük were either blocked or throttled for four days. Officials ne er confi med the restrictions, instead stating that the outage was due to a cyberattack.[38]

---

29 Efe Kerem Sozeri, "Turkey Blocks News Sites, Twitter, Facebook After Deadly Attack," June 28, 2016, http://www.vocativ.com/334890/turkey-blocks-news-sites-twitter-facebook-after-deadly-attack/

30 Julia Carrie Wong, "Social media may have been blocked during Turkey coup attempt," July 15, 2016, https://www.theguardian.com/world/2016/jul/15/turkey-blocking-social-facebook-twitter-youtube

31 Turkey Blocks, "Social media blocked in Turkey following Gaziantep blast," August 21, 2016, https://turkeyblocks.org/2016/08/21/social-media-blocked-turkey-following-gaziantep-blast/

32 Turkey Blocks, "Social media blocked in Turkey," August 25, 2016, https://turkeyblocks.org/2016/08/25/social-media-blocked-turkey/

33 May Bulman, "Facebook, Twitter and Whatsapp blocked in Turkey after arrest of opposition leaders," Independent, November 4, 2016, http://www.independent.co.uk/news/world/asia/facebook-twitter-whatsapp-turkey-Erdoğan-blocked-opposition-leaders-arrested-a7396831.html

34 "Turkey blocks access to Facebook, Twitter and WhatsApp following ambassador's assassination," The Telegraph, December 20, 2016, http://www.telegraph.co.uk/technology/2016/12/20/turkey-blocks-access-facebook-twitter-whatsapp-following-ambassadors/

35 Ankara First Judgeship of Peace decision dated December 20, 2016, https://www.lumendatabase.org/file_upl_ads/files/4159952/004/159/952/original/Ankara_3_d_Criminal_Judgeship_of_Peace_2016-6929_Misc.-_Lumen.pdf

36 Turkey Blocks, "News site of Dutch Broadcast Foundation NOS blocked in Turkey," December 21, 2016, https://turkeyblocks.org/2016/12/21/nos-dutch-broadcast-foundation-blocked-in-turkey/

37 Turkey Blocks, "Social media shutdowns in Turkey after ISIS releases soldier video," December 23, 2016, https://turkeyblocks.org/2016/12/23/social-media-shutdowns-turkey-isis-releases-soldier-video/

38 Fusun S. Nebil, "Elinin Hamuru ile Siber Saldırı Haberi mi?," Turk-Internet, December 27, 2016, http://www.turk-internet.com/portal/yazigoster.php?yaziid=54927

TURKEY

On October 8, 2016, Dropbox, OneDrive, GitHub, Google Drive, and Internet Archive were temporarily blocked after they were used by hackers to host 17 GB of leaked government emails. The documents were obtained by RedHack, a Turkish Marxist-Leninist hacker group, from the private account of Berat Albayrak, the energy minister and President Erdoğan's son-in-law.[39] The BTK banned news regarding the leak, and Twitter banned the accounts of RedHack. In a separate incident, Turkey blocked access to WikiLeaks after nearly 300,000 emails from the AKP were indexed on the website.[40]

In November 2016, the BTK order ISPs to ban more than 10 VPN services,[41] as well as the circumvention tool Tor.[42] In May 2017, Wikipedia was blocked in the country. The ban was approved by Ankara's 1st Criminal Court in order to prevent access to two articles, "Foreign Involvement in the Syrian Civil War" and "State-Sponsored Terrorism," that mentioned the Turkish government's involvement in Syria.[43]

The blocking and removal of online content (see "Content Removal" below) is regulated under Law No. 5651, whose full name is "Regulation of Publications on the Internet and Suppression of Crimes Committed by Means of Such Publication."[44] It was initially enacted in 2007 to protect children and prevent access to illegal and harmful internet content. This includes material related to child sexual abuse, drug use, the provision of dangerous substances, prostitution, obscenity, gambling, suicide promotion, and crimes against Mustafa Kemal Atatürk, the founder of the Republic of Turkey.[45] The responsibilities of content providers, hosting companies, public access providers, and ISPs are delineated in Law No. 5651. Domestically hosted websites with proscribed content can be taken down, while websites based abroad can be blocked and fil ered through ISPs. The law has already been found to be in contravention of the European Convention on Human Rights.

In December 2015, the European Court of Human Rights ruled that the blocking of YouTube in 2008 violated Article 10 of the European Convention on Human Rights, specifically the right o freedom of expression. The case was brought to the court by law professors Yaman Akdeniz and Kerem Altıparmak, as well as lawyer Serkan Cengiz.[46]

Law No. 5651 has repeatedly been amended in recent years to broaden the scope for censorship.[47] A set of amendments enacted in March 2015 authorized cabinet ministers to order the TİB to block

39   Efe Kerem Sozeri, "How hacktivist group RedHack gamed Turkey's censorship regime," October 12, 2016, https://www.dailydot.com/layer8/redhack-gamed-turkey-censorship/

40   Kareem Shaheen, "Turkey blocks access to WikiLeaks after Erdoğan party emails go online," The Guardian, July 20, 2016, https://www.theguardian.com/world/2016/jul/20/turkey-blocks-access-to-wikileaks-after-Erdogan-party-emails-go-online

41   Efe Kerem Sozeri, "Activists fight ack against Turkish government s block on Tor and VPNs," November 6, 2016, https://www.dailydot.com/layer8/turkey-block-tor-vpns-activists/

42   Lorenzo Franceschi-Bicchierai, "Turkey Doubles Down on Censorship With Block on VPNs, Tor," Vice, November 4, 2016, https://motherboard.vice.com/en_us/article/turkey-doubles-down-on-censorship-with-block-on-vpns-tor

43   Efe Kerem Sözeri, "Inside Turkey's war on Wikipedia," May 9, 2017, https://www.dailydot.com/layer8/turkey-bans-wikipedia-censorship/

44   Law No. 5651 was published in the Official Gazette on May 23, 2007, in issue No. 26030. A copy of the law can be found (in Turkish) at World Intellectual Property Organization, "Law No. 5651 on Regulating Broadcasting in the Internet and Fighting Against Crimes Committed through Internet Broadcasting," http://www.wipo.int/wipolex/en/details.jsp?id=11035 ; Telekomunikasyon Iletisim Baskanligi (TIB), "Information about the regulations of the content of the Internet," in "Frequently Asked Questions," http://bit.ly/1PtuhBN

45   Human Rights Watch, "Turkey: Internet Freedom, Rights in Sharp Decline," September 2, 2014, http://bit.ly/1r1klQF

46   "Human rights court rules block on YouTube violated freedom of expression," Today's Zaman, December 1, 2015, http://www.todayszaman.com/anasayfa_human-rights-court-rules-block-on-youtube-violated-freedom-of-expression_405790.html

47   World Intellectual Property Organization, "Law No.5651 on Regulating Broadcasting in the Internet and Fighting Against Crimes Committed through Internet Broadcasting," May 4, 2007, http://www.wipo.int/wipolex/en/details.jsp?id=11035

content when necessary to "defend the right to life, secure property, ensure national security and public order, prevent crime, or protect public health." The orders are then taken up within four hours by the TİB (now the BTK after the TİB's closure in 2016), which must also submit the decision to a criminal court within 24 hours. If a judge does not validate the decision within 48 hours, the blocking order must be rescinded.[48] A similar bill passed in September 2014 had been overturned by the Constitutional Court in October of that year. While the original version of Law No. 5651 included only notice-based liability and takedown provisions for content that violates individual rights, changes passed in February 2014 extended this provision to include URL-based blocking orders to be issued by a criminal court judge. The February 2014 amendments also entrusted the TİB with broad discretion to block content that an individual or other legal claimant perceives as a violation of privacy, while failing to establish strong checks and balances. These changes came after leaks of the alleged phone conversations of top government officials on December 17, 2013, and they laid the groundwork for the eventual blocking of social media platforms.

The February 2014 amendments to Law No. 5651 also shielded TİB staff if they committed crimes during the exercise of their duties. Criminal investigations into TİB staff could only be initiated through an authorization from the TİB director, and investigations into the director could only be initiated by the relevant minister. This process cast serious doubt on the functioning and accountability of the TİB.

ISPs must join an Association for Access Providers in order to obtain an "activity certifica e" to legally operate in the country. ISPs must also comply with blocking orders from the BTK within four hours or face a penalty of up to TRY 300,000 (US$80,000). Failure to take measures to block all alternative means of accessing the targeted site, such as proxy sites, may result in a fine f up to TRY 50,000 (US$13,000).[49]

The vast majority of blocking orders have been issued by the TİB and its successor the BTK,[50] rather than by the courts.[51] The procedures surrounding blocking decisions are opaque in both cases, creating significant challenges for those seeking o appeal. Judges can issue blocking orders during preliminary investigations as well as during trials. The reasoning behind court decisions is not provided in blocking notices, and the relevant rulings are not easily accessible. As a result, it is often difficult for si e owners to determine why their site has been blocked and which court has issued the order. The BTK's mandate includes executing judicial blocking orders, but it can also issue administrative orders for foreign websites, content involving sexual abuse of children, and obscenity. Moreover, in some cases it successfully asks content and hosting providers to remove offending items from their servers, in order to avoid issuing a blocking order that would affect an entire website. This occurs despite the fact that intermediaries are not responsible for third-party content on their sites. The fil ering database is maintained by the government without clear criteria. A "Child

---

48   "Approved article gives Turkish gov't power to shut down websites in four hours," *Hurriyet Daily News*, March 20, 2015, http://bit.ly/1C3iuA8

49   For further information on this section, see Representative on Freedom of the Media, "Briefing on P oposed Amendments to Law No. 5651," Organization for Security and Co-operation in Europe, January 2014, http://bit.ly/1X3Z4az ; Center for Internet and Society, Stanford Law School, "WILMAP: Turkey," accessed November 6, 2014, http://stanford.io/1YcNBEX

50   Engelli Web, "Kurum Bazinda Istatistikler," accessed February 28, 2016, http://engelliweb.com/istatistikler/

51   According to TİB statistics from May 2009, the last date these were available, the courts are responsible for 21 percent of blocked websites, while 79 percent are blocked administratively by the TİB. Reporters Without Borders, "Telecom Authority Accused of Concealing Blocked Website Figures," May 19, 2010, http://en.rsf.org/turkey-telecom-authority-accused-of-19-05-2010.37511.html

---

TURKEY

and Family Profiles Cri eria Working Committee" was introduced to address this problem in 2012, but it was largely made up of BTK members or appointees and does not appear to be active.

In addition to these blocks, ISPs offer "child" and "family" fil ering options under rules established by the BTK in 2011, though the fil ering criteria have been criticized as arbitrary and discriminatory.[52] The BTK tried to mandate fil ering for all users in 2011,[53] but withdrew the proposal following a legal challenge.[54] The child fil er obstructs access to Facebook, YouTube, Yasam Radyo (Life Radio), the Armenian minority newspaper *Agos*, and several websites advocating the theory of evolution,[55] even as some antievolution websites remain accessible.[56] Internet access is fil ered at primary education institutions and public bodies, resulting in the blocking of a number of minority news sites.[57]

Content Removal

In addition to widespread fil ering, state authorities are proactive in requesting the deletion or removal of content. Social media platforms comply with administrative decisions and court orders as promptly as possible in order to avoid blocking and, more recently, throttling. Like international social media platforms, popular Turkish websites are subject to content removal orders. Courts issued several orders pertaining to user-generated content websites such as Ekşi Sözlük (Sour Dictionary), İnci Sözlük (Pearl Dictionary), and İTÜ Sözlük (Istanbul Technical University Dictionary).

Turkey has consistently ranked among the countries with the highest number of removal requests sent to Twitter. Turkey accounted for 65 percent of all accounts reported to Twitter for the period of June 2016 to May 2017. The company withheld at least some content in 11 percent of the removal requests in the fi st half of 2017.[58] It explained, "Whenever possible under Turkish law, Twitter filed legal objections in esponse to all court orders involving journalists and news outlets.... Disappointingly, none of our objections prevailed."[59]

According to Facebook's Government Requests Report for the period of July to December 2016, the company restricted 1,111 pieces of content on orders from both the BTK and Turkish law enforcement agencies, particularly in compliance with Law No. 5651.[60] Figures from Reddit indicate that it complied with all six requests it received from the Turkish government in 2016, resulting in the blocking of one post and fi e subreddits for Turkish IP addresses.[61] The requests related to

52   Reporters Without Borders, "New Internet Filtering System Condemned as Backdoor Censorship," December 2, 2011, http://bit.ly/1W3FNp7

53   Decision No. 2011/DK-10/91 of Bilgi Teknolojileri ve İletişim Kurumu, dated February 22, 2011.

54   On September 27, 2011, the Council of State rejected the "stay of execution" request by BIAnet referring to the annulment of the February 22, 2011.

55   Dorian Jones, "Turkey Blocks Web Pages Touting Darwin's Evolution Theory," Voice of America, December 23, 2011. http://bit.ly/1Lh9DmR

56   Sara Reardon, "Controversial Turkish Internet Censorship Program Targets Evolution Sites." *Science Magazine*. December 9, 2011, http://bit.ly/1Ofyitl ; Haber Merkezi, "Agos'u Biz Değil Sistem Engelledi," [Agos was fil ered through the Ministry of Education fil er], *BIAnet*, January 23, 2012, http://bit.ly/1jzOWr4

57   "Meclis'te Alevi Sitesine Yanlışlıkla Sansür," *BIAnet*, December 8, 2014, http://bit.ly/1FNfbzb

58   Twitter, "Turkey," *Transparency Report* https://transparency.twitter.com/en/removal-requests.html#removal-requests-jan-jun-2017

59   "Turkey leads in social media censorship: new Twitter transparency report." Turkey Blocks, March 21, 2017, https://turkeyblocks.org/2017/03/21/turkey-leads-social-media-censorship-new-twitter-transparency-report/

60   Facebook, "Turkey," *Government Requests Report*, July to December 2015, accessed October 15, 2016, https://govtrequests.facebook.com/country/Turkey/2015-H2/#

61   "Transparency Report," Reddit, April 2017, https://www.reddit.com/wiki/transparency/2016

content deemed "obscene" under Turkish law. Although Reddit did not reveal the nature of the content, researchers discovered that some of the subreddits related to LGBTI-friendly sections of the website.[62]

Media, Diversity, and Content Manipulation

Digital media are inhibited by self-censorship, government manipulation, and shutdowns of independent outlets. A steep rise in prosecutions under the charge of defaming the president has also had a chilling effect on social media users. This has been compounded by decrees passed under the state of emergency that have expanded surveillance. Turkish-Armenian relations have become less controversial in recent years, but they remain sensitive, particularly during periods of ethnic tension and violence in the southeast.

Turkish users increasingly rely on internet-based publications as a primary source of news, despite the country's restrictive legal environment and growing self-censorship. There are a wide range of blogs and websites through which citizens question and criticize Turkish politics and leaders, though many such platforms have been blocked since the attempted coup and the fla e-up in hostilities between government forces and Kurdish separatists. The November 2016 blocking of Tor and popular VPN services made it more difficult for use s to reach blocked websites.[63]

In addition, several well-known news outlets have been taken over or shut down by the authorities. The Gülen-linked newspapers *Zaman* and *Today's Zaman*, as well as Cihan News Agency, were seized on March 4, 2017. New progovernment editorial boards were established by court order.[64] The online archives of each paper were deleted, as was *Zaman*'s previous Twitter activity.[65] *Zaman* and some 130 other news companies had been shut down on July 27, 2016, by Decree No. 668, immediately after the government arrested 89 media workers for alleged ties to the Gülen movement.[66]

As of mid-2017, the progovernment newspaper *Sabah* had the most visited news site in the country, followed by *Haber7* and *Ensonhaber*.[67] New models for citizen journalism and volunteer reporting have recently gained traction; examples include 140journos, dokuz8haber, and *Ötekilerin Postası*, whose editor was arrested in November 2015. Media coverage regarding the Kurdish-populated southeastern region is heavily influenced by the go ernment. Frequent power outages, mobile internet shutdowns, and censorship of prominent local news sites make information gathering even more difficult in that a ea.

---

62   "LGBTI sections disappear as Reddit complies with 100% of Turkey censorship orders," Turkey Blocks, April 4, 2017, https://turkeyblocks.org/2017/04/04/lgbti-sections-disappear-as-reddit-complies-with-turkey-censorship-orders/

63   Fusun S. Nebil, "BTK'nın VPN Engelleme Israr Devam Ediyor," Turk-Internet, December 5, 2016, http://www.turk-internet.com/portal/yazigoster.php?yaziid=54731

64   "Zaman newspaper: Seized Turkish daily 'now pro-government'," BBC News, March 6, 2016, http://www.bbc.com/news/world-europe-35739547; "Istanbul court to appoint trustees for Zaman, Today's Zaman editorial board," Committee to Protect Journalists, March 4, 2016, https://cpj.org/2016/03/istanbul-court-to-appoint-trustees-for-zaman-today.php

65   Zaman's Twitter account has been renamed "@AnalizMerkez," See to Efe Kerem Sozeri's statement: https://twitter.com/efekerem/status/706282702861942784?lang=en and https://web.archive.org/web/20160306005700/https:/twitter.com/analizmerkez

66   "Turkey: Media Shut Down, Journalists Detained," Human Rights Watch, July 28, 2016, https://www.hrw.org/news/2016/07/28/turkey-media-shut-down-journalists-detained

67   See "Turkey," Alexa, accessed October 2017, https://www.alexa.com/topsites/countries/TR

TURKEY

Numerous reports have revealed that an "army of trolls,"[68] numbering around 6,000 individuals, has been enlisted by the ruling AKP to manipulate discussions, drive particular agendas, and combat government critics on social media.[69] Emails leaked in October 2016 (see "Technical Attacks") provided insight into a coordinated campaign by President Erdoğan's inner circle to counter critical narratives and weaken protest movements on social media.[70] Messages sent to Berat Albayrak discussed the establishment of "a team of professional graphic designers, coders, and former army officials who eceived training in psychological warfare," according to a report by the *Daily Dot*. One email proposed exposing the drug habits of celebrities who had supported the 2013 Occupy Gezi movement, resulting in a police raid on the homes of 55 actors, directors, and other celebrities two months later. The images of the celebrities were widely shared by progovernment outlets on social media. Also using social media, an AKP lawmaker rallied an angry mob to physically attack the headquarters of *Hurriyet* in September 2015 after the newspaper criticized President Erdoğan's security policy.[71]

Journalists and scholars who are critical of the government have faced orchestrated harassment on Twitter, often by dozens or even hundreds of users.[72] Shortly before the November 2015 elections, progovernment trolls circulated allegations that Oy ve Ötesi (Vote and Beyond), the fi st civic election-monitoring initiative in Turkey, was committing fraud and aiding terrorist organizations. A Twitter account named "Vote and Fraud" with 42,000 followers warned supporters not to get involved with the group. Only a week before the smear campaign, the same account had purported to be a young girl sharing romantic quotes, adding to speculation that "Vote and Fraud" was a fake account created solely for the purposes of trolling.[73] Progovernment trolls have also been active amid rapid shifts in relations with foreign governments, such as Russia, which commenced a propaganda campaign against Turkey after Turkish forces shot down a Russian jet near the Syrian border in December 2015. In response, "TrollState Russia" became a trending topic on Twitter in a campaign allegedly orchestrated by Erdoğan's public communication office .[74]

Digital Activism

Digital activism has played a significant ole in the country since the 2013 Occupy Gezi protests, although activism has waned somewhat as a result of the repressive climate after the coup attempt. Ten activists—eight Turkish human rights activists and two foreign trainers—were detained while participating in a digital security workshop at a hotel in Istanbul in July 2017.[75] The individuals

68   Dion Nissembaum, "Before Turkish Coup, President's Drive to Stifle Dissent So ed Unrest," *The Wall Street Journal*, July 15, 2016, http://www.wsj.com/articles/before-turkish-coup-presidents-drive-to-stifle-dissen -sowed-unrest-1468632017

69   "CHP asks if pro-gov't trolls put on AK Party payroll," *Cihan*, September 4, 2014, http://bit.ly/1UWSep1

70   Efe Kerem Sozeri, "RedHack leaks reveal the rise of Turkey's pro-government Twitter trolls," *The Daily Dot*, September 30, 2016, http://www.dailydot.com/layer8/redhack-turkey-albayrak-censorship/

71   Efe Kerem Sozeri, "RedHack leaks reveal the rise of Turkey's pro-government Twitter trolls," *The Daily Dot*, September 30, 2016, http://www.dailydot.com/layer8/redhack-turkey-albayrak-censorship/

72   Emre Kizilkaya, "AKP's social media wars," *Al Monitor*, November 15, 2013, http://bit.ly/1LhdTCG

73   Efe Kerem Sozeri, "How pro-government trolls are using a sexy Twitter bot to sway Turkey's election, " *Daily Dot*, October 31, 2015, http://www.dailydot.com/politics/turkey-election-twitter-troll-vote-and-beyond-vote-and-fraud/

74   Efe Kerem Sozeri, "Inside the great troll war between Russia and Turkey, " *Daily Dot*, December 14, 2015, http://www.dailydot.com/politics/russia-turkey-missle-turkey-troll-war-twitter/

75   Aria Bendix, "Turkish Police Detain Activists on Suspicion of Terrorist Affiliations" *The Atlantic*, July 6, 2017, https://www.theatlantic.com/news/archive/2017/07/turkish-police-detain-rights-activists-on-suspicion-of-terrorism/532851/

included İdil Eser, director of Amnesty International's Turkey branch. As of mid-2017, they were awaiting trial on trumped-up charges of aiding a terrorist group.[76]

Turkey Blocks, an organization that tracks censorship in real time, was granted Index on Censorship's 2017 award for digital activism.[77] Organizations such as Oy ve Ötesi used social media tools to enlist over 60,000 volunteers to monitor more than 130,000 ballot boxes during the general elections of November 2015.[78] Operations were scaled back for the 2017 constitutional referendum over fears of legal repercussions for their members.[79] Oy ve Ötesi later published a report about irregularities affecting around 100,000 ballots.[80] Dogruluk Payi ("Share of Truth"), Turkey's fi st and only political fact-checking website, was also a popular source for information during the coverage period.[81]

Violations of User Rights

While prison sentences for online speech have been rare, several individuals were sentenced to lengthy terms over the past year for allegedly insulting public officials or spreading terrorist propaganda. Journalists, public figures, and students have been targeted for nonviolent speech that is critical of the government or touches on controversial issues like Kurdish identity. Surveillance remains a key concern, but cybersecurity made headlines over the past year due to a massive leak of a government official's emails.

Legal Environment

The state of emergency, in place since July 20, 2016, weakens parliamentary and constitutional checks on executive decrees issued by President Erdoğan and his cabinet. Decrees have been used to arrest over 50,000 people allegedly linked to the coup attempt, suspend or dismiss over 140,000 individuals from their jobs, block websites, shut down communication networks, and close civil society organizations and news outlets.[82] Decree No. 671, published on August 15, 2016, amended the Law on Digital Communications to authorize the government to take "any necessary measure" on the grounds of "national security, public order, prevention of crime, protection of public health and public morals, or protection of the rights and freedoms" guaranteed under Article 22 of the

76   Aria Bendix, "Turkish Court Jails Human-Rights Activists," *The Atlantic*, July 18, 2017, https://www.theatlantic.com/news/archive/2017/07/turkish-court-jails-human-rights-activists/534105/

77   "Digital Activism 2017," Index on Censorship, April 20, 2017, https://www.indexoncensorship.org/2017/04/digital-activism-2017/

78   Oy ve Ötesi Derneği, "Seçim Sonuç Değerlendirmeleri" [in Turkish], news release, June 10, 2015, http://oyveotesi.org/3-kasim-2015-genel-secimleri/1-kasim-2015-secim-sonuc-degerlendirmeleri/

79   Laura Pitel, "Turkey referendum monitor: "It is a very, very different climate and a different environment to the last elections," Medium, April 14, 2017, https://medium.com/@Pitel/turkey-referendum-monitor-it-is-a-very-very-different-climate-and-a-different-environment-to-the-cf5c62ffe1e3

80   "Vote and Beyond Election Monitoring Organization Releases Report on Referendum," BIA News Desk, April 21, 2017, http://bianet.org/english/human-rights/185785-vote-and-beyond-election-monitoring-organization-releases-report-on-referendum?bia_source=rss

81   Riada Ašimović Akyol, "Will new Turkish fact-checking site be able to hold politicians accountable?," *Al Monitor*, February 3, 2016, http://www.al-monitor.com/pulse/originals/2016/02/turkey-politics-meet-fact-checking.html#

82   Patrick Kingsley, "Erdoğan Says He Will Extend His Sweeping Rule Over Turkey," *New York Times*, May 21, 2017, https://www.nytimes.com/2017/05/21/world/europe/turkey-Erdoğan-state-of-emergency.html?_r=0. See also, Turkey Purge, https://turkeypurge.com/

constitution. The decree also obliges telecommunications providers to enforce government orders within two hours of receiving them.[83]

The Turkish constitution includes broad protections for freedom of expression. Article 26 states that "everyone has the right to express and disseminate his thought and opinion by speech, in writing or in pictures or through other media, individually or collectively."[84] Turkish legislation and court judgments are subject to the European Convention on Human Rights and bound by the decisions of the European Court of Human Rights. The constitution also seeks to guarantee the right to privacy, though there are limitations on the use of encryption devices, and surveillance by security agencies is believed to be widespread. There are no laws that specifically criminalize online activities li e posting one's opinions, downloading information, sending email, or transmitting text messages. Instead, many provisions of the criminal code and other laws, such as the Anti-Terrorism Law, are applied to both online and offline activit .

Defamation charges have frequently been used to prosecute government critics. According to Article 125 of the Turkish criminal code, "anyone who undermines the honor, dignity or respectability of another person or who attacks a person's honor by attributing to them a concrete act or a fact, or by means of an insult, shall be sentenced to imprisonment for a term of three months to two years, or punished with a judicial fine" Defaming a public official carries a minimum one- ear sentence, while insulting the president entails a sentence of one to four years in prison, according to Article 299. Several courts deemed Article 299 unconstitutional in the fi st half of 2016 and called for the matter to be taken up by the Constitutional Court.[85] Cases related to insulting the president have seldom resulted in jail sentences, although some defendants have been jailed while awaiting trial.

According to Article 7 of the Anti-Terrorism Law, "those who make propaganda of a terrorist organization by legitimizing, glorifying or inciting violent methods or threats" are liable to prison terms of one to fi e years. The law has been widely criticized for its broad definition f terrorism, which has been exploited by courts to prosecute journalists and academics with no link to terrorism for the simple act of criticizing the government.[86]

Prosecutions and Detentions for Online Activities

The past year featured an unprecedented increase in the number of prosecutions and detentions of Turkish citizens for their online activities.

Tens of thousands of Turkish citizens have been arbitrarily detained for their alleged use of the encrypted communications app ByLock. Legal and technical experts have disputed the government's claim that the app was primarily used by members of the Gülen movement, pointing to its wide availability and popularity in 41 countries. It was once available to download at no cost on the app

83   Efe Kerem Sozeri, "Turkey uses emergency decree to shut down internet on 11 Kurdish cities to 'prevent protests'," *The Daily Dot,* October 27, 2016, https://www.dailydot.com/layer8/turkey-cuts-kurdistan-internet/

84   The Constitution of the Republic of Turkey, accessed April 22, 2013, https://global.tbmm.gov.tr/docs/constitution_en.pdf

85   "Local court applies to Turkey's top court to annul article on 'insulting president'," *Hurriyet Daily News,* March 30, 2016, http://www.hurriyetdailynews.com/local-court-applies-to-turkeys-top-court-to-annul-insulting-president-law. aspx?pageID=238&nID=97103&NewsCatID=509

86   "Why Turkey's terror law is the 'Achilles heel' of the EU-Turkey visa deal," France 24, May 13, 2016, http://www.france24. com/en/20160513-why-turkeys-terror-law-achilles-heel-eu-turkey-migrant-deal

TURKEY

stores of Apple and Google, until it was removed by the developer.[87] Turkish officials claim that the app was designed by a senior member of the Gülen movement. Experts believe that Turkey's National Intelligence Organization (MİT) hacked a ByLock server located in Lithuania, which listed its hundreds of thousands of users in an unencrypted form. Despite a lack of evidence, and the arbitrary nature of the blanket arrests, numerous users have been deemed guilty by association for simply downloading the app. In the month of October 2016 alone, arrest warrants were issued for 404 individuals for allegedly using ByLock, including members of the police and judiciary.[88]

The ByLock controversy has also ensnared members of the human rights community. Taner Kılıç, the Turkey chair of Amnesty International, was detained in June 2017, and the only known evidence in his case was the allegation that he had used ByLock, which he has denied.

One month later, police arrested 10 human rights activists taking part in a digital security training in Istanbul. Turkish citizens İdil Eser, Günal Kurşun, Özlem Dalkıran, Veli Acu, İlknur Üstün, and Nalan Erkem were placed in pretrial detention, as were their trainers, German citizen Peter Steudtner and Swedish citizen Ali Gharavi. Şeyhmus Özbekli and Nejat Taştan were arrested and released on bail. They all face prison sentences of up to 15 years for membership in a terrorist organization.[89]

Arrests and prosecutions for social media posts have increased in recent years, and in some cases, individuals have been imprisoned. Over the past year, hundreds of Twitter users faced charges of insulting government officials, defaming P esident Erdoğan, or sharing propaganda in support of terrorist organizations.

According to the Committee to Protect Journalists, a total of 81 journalists were imprisoned in Turkey as of December 2016.[90] Several journalists were charged for their social media activities, including but not limited to the following individuals:

- Journalist Hayri Tunç, who works for the news site Jiyan, was sentenced to two years in prison in June 2016 for "terrorism propaganda," "abetting criminal acts," and "glorifying criminal acts." He was targeted for tweets, Facebook posts, and YouTube videos that mainly covered fighting bet een the security services and Kurdish militants.[91] He appealed the decision shortly after his sentencing.[92]

- Ahmet Şık, a leading investigative journalist with the opposition outlet *Cumhuriyet*, was arrested for his social media activity in December 2016. He was accused of "spreading

87   Owen Bowcott, "Turks detained for using encrypted app 'had human rights breached'," *The Guardian*, September 11, 2017, https://www.theguardian.com/world/2017/sep/11/turks-detained-encrypted-bylock-messaging-app-human-rights-breached

88   Umar Farooq, "In Turkey, you can be arrested for having this app on your phone," *LA Times*, October 19, 2016, http://www.latimes.com/world/europe/la-fg-turkey-purge-crackdown-snap-story.html

89   "Eyes of the world on Turkey as show trial of human rights activists begins," Amnesty International, October 25, 2017, https://www.amnesty.org/en/latest/news/2017/10/eyes-of-the-world-on-turkey-as-show-trial-of-human-rights-activists-begins/

90   "2016 prison census: 259 journalists jailed worldwide," Committee to Protect Journalists, 2017, https://cpj.org/imprisoned/2016.php

91   Efe Kerem Sozeri, "Kurdish Reporter Faces Jail Time in Turkey for Twitter and Facebook Posts, " *Global Voices*, March 9, 2016, https://globalvoices.org/2016/03/09/kurdish-reporter-faces-jail-time-in-turkey-for-twitter-and-facebook-posts/

92   "Gazeteci Hayri Tunç'a 2 yıl hapis cezası!," *Birgun*, June 7, 2016, http://www.birgun.net/haber-detay/gazeteci-hayri-tunc-a-2-yil-hapis-cezasi-115140.html

terrorist propaganda" and "denigrating the Turkish Republic."[93] He claimed he was denied drinking water for three days while in custody.[94]

- In September 2015, journalist and writer Aytekin Gezici received a combined prison sentence of fi e years and nine months, in addition to a judicial fine equi alent to 21 months in prison, for "insulting" President Erdoğan, former deputy prime minister Bülent Arınç, and former justice minister Bekir Bozdağ on Twitter.[95] He was acquitted of similar charges against two other public officials. Gezici had been detained in Oc ober 2014 in Adana after a police raid on his home.[96] Although he was not immediately imprisoned (likely due to an appeal), he was again detained in July 2016 for alleged links to the failed coup.[97]

- Hüsnü Mahalli was arrested in December 2016 on charges of insulting the president and defaming public officials a ter he criticized Turkish media's coverage of the Syrian conflict. Mahalli, a journalist and political analyst, was born in Syria but acquired Turkish citizenship in 2011.[98]

- Beatriz Yubero, a Spanish journalist who had been performing research on IS at Ankara University, was taken into custody over tweets she posted about President Erdoğan. She was deported on August 6, 2016.[99]

- Atilla Taş, an eccentric singer and *Meydan* columnist, was arrested in September 2016 on suspicion of membership of a terrorist organization.[100] The evidence used in his case included a tweet in which he stated, "Edison wouldn't have invented the 'light bulb' if he saw these days!" in a reference to the AKP's "light bulb" logo. He was released in March, only to be detained once again by another judge.[101]

Authorities have also targeted ordinary citizens and university students for their social media activity. Gizem Yerik, a 23-year-old fine a ts student, was sentenced to a combined four years and eight months in prison for allegedly insulting the president and spreading terrorist propaganda on Twitter. Her sentence was confi med by the Supreme Court of Appeals in May 2017.[102] In April, police arrested Ali Gul, a 22-year-old university student, for sharing a popular video calling on Turkish

---

93   "Turkish journalist Ahmet Sik held 'over tweet'," BBC, December 29, 2016, http://www.bbc.com/news/world-europe-38457798

94   "Imprisoned Turkish journalist denied drinking water for three days," PEN America, January 6, 2017, https://pen.org/press-release/imprisoned-turkish-journalist-denied-water-for-three-days/

95   "Gazeteci Aytekin Gezici'ye Erdoğan'a hakareten 6 yıl hapis," *Birgün*, September 17, 2015, http://bit.ly/1Lb26UR

96   "Turkey's journalists challenged by growing judicial, political pressure," *Today's Zaman*, May 28, 2015, http://bit.ly/1iPzx61

97   Gündem Haberi, "Aytekin Gezici tutuklandı, Yüksel Evsen Adli Kontrolle serbest...," Ajans Adana, July 25, 2016, http://ajansadana.com/haber-8406-aytekin_gezici_tutuklandi._yuksel_evsen_adli_kontrolle_serbest...html

98   Efe Kerem Sozeri, "Turkey ramps up war on free speech with latest arrest of a journalist," *Daily Dot*, December 16, 2016, https://www.dailydot.com/layer8/turkey-arrest-husnu-mahalli/

99   "Spanish journalist 'deported over tweets'," *Hurriyet Daily News*, August 8, 2016, http://www.hurriyetdailynews.com/Default.aspx?pageID=238&nID=102627&NewsCatID=341

100   "Singer and Columnist Atilla Taş: "I was arrested by a judge like you," *Washington Hatti*, December 27, 2016, http://washingtonhatti.com/2017/03/31/singer-and-columnist-atilla-tas-i-was-arrested-by-a-judge-like-you/

101   Safak Pavey, "Inside Erdoğan's Prisons," *New York Times*, July 14, 2017, https://www.nytimes.com/2017/07/14/opinion/turkey-Erdoğan-prison.html

102   "Üniversite öğrencisi Gizem Yerik'e hapis cezası," HaberTurk, May 13, 2016, http://www.haberturk.com/gundem/haber/1238957-universite-ogrencisi-gizem-yerike-hapis-cezasi

---

citizens to vote "No" in the constitutional referendum. He received a two-year suspended sentence and was released in May.[103]

President Erdoğan has reportedly filed criminal complaints against mo e than 250 people for "insulting" him online and more than 2,000 people for "insulting" him by any means from 2014 to 2016.[104] Speaking on July 30, 2016, after the failed coup, Erdoğan announced that he would withdraw all pending insult complaints.[105] Nevertheless, Article 125(3) and Article 299 of the penal code remained in place, and new cases continued to be filed during the co erage period.

Surveillance, Privacy, and Anonymity

Government surveillance, the bulk retention of user data, and limitations on encryption and anonymity are all concerns in Turkey. Leaked emails revealed a contract between the Italian surveillance software company Hacking Team and the General Directorate of Security (GDS), a civilian police force, for the use of Hacking Team's "Remote Control System" from June 2011 to November 2014.[106] Under Turkish law, the interception of electronic communications had fallen under the purview of the TİB (now the BTK), and questions remain over the legality of the GDS using software that can infiltra e targets' computers. The prominence of alleged Gülenists in the police and judiciary had been a major point of discussion in the country in recent years, particularly after Gülenists were widely blamed for leaked wiretaps that led to various government corruption scandals in 2013 and 2014. Further scandals prompted high-level dismissals and reshuffling within the police and judiciary, apparently aimed at removing suspected Gülenist officials [107] The 2016 coup attempt prompted a new wave of surveillance as part of the broader purge of individuals with alleged links to banned groups. Almost 70,000 social media accounts have been put under surveillance since July 2016, according to figu es reported in January 2017.[108]

According to Article 22 of the constitution, "everyone has the right to freedom of communication, and secrecy of communication is fundamental." This right can only be violated under a court order in cases of "national security, public order, prevention of the commission of crimes, protection of public health and public morals, or protection of the rights and freedoms of others, or unless there exists a written order of an agency authorized by law in cases where delay is prejudicial."[109] For the most part, any action that could interfere with freedom of communication or the right to privacy must be authorized by the judiciary. For example, judicial permission is required for technical surveillance under the Penal Procedural Law. Before the passage of the Homeland Security Act in March 2015, the law allowed Turkish security forces to conduct intelligence wiretapping for 24 hours without a judge's permission in urgent situations. However, under the new law the time limit was increased

---

103   Can Dundar, "The high price of saying 'no' in Turkey's referendum", *Washington Post*, April13, 2017, https://www. washingtonpost.com/news/democracy-post/wp/2017/04/13/the-high-price-of-saying-no-in-turkeys-referendum/?utm term=.05c26d2b1742

104   Finkel, "Miss Turkey on Trial for Allegedly Insulting President Erdoğan." and "Cumhurbaskanina Hakaret Davalarinda Patlama" in Turkish, *Aktif Haber*, November 22, 2015, http://www.aktifhaber.com/cumhurbaskanina-hakaret-davalarinda-patlama-1263244h.htm

105   "President Erdoğan withdrawing lawsuits filed for insult" *Hurriyet Daily News*, July 30, 2016, http://www.hurriyetdailynews. com/president-Erdoğan-withdrawing-lawsuits-filed-fo -insult.aspx?pageID=238&nID=102278&NewsCatID=338

106   Efe Kerem Sözeri, "Turkey paid Hacking Team $600k to spy on civilians," *The Daily Dot*, July 7, 2015. http://www.dailydot. com/politics/hacking-team-turkey/

107   "Turkish court accepts indictment of TIB over illegal spying," *TRT World*, June 2, 2015, http://bit.ly/1EgTTyZ

108   "Over 68K social media accounts under police surveillance in Turkey," *Birgun*, January 17, 2017, http://www.birgun.net/ haber-detay/over-68k-social-media-accounts-under-police-surveillance-in-turkey-143122.html

109   The Constitution of the Republic of Turkey.

---

to 48 hours, with a new requirement that wiretapping officials noti y their superiors. In addition, only the Ankara High Criminal Court is authorized to decide whether the wiretapping is legitimate. Despite constitutional guarantees, most forms of telecommunication continue to be tapped and intercepted.[110]

Furthermore, the MİT received expanded powers to conduct surveillance in April 2014. Law No. 6532 on Amending the Law on State Intelligence Services and the National Intelligence Organization grants intelligence agents unfettered access to communications data without a court order. The law forces public and private bodies—including but not limited to banks, archives, private companies, and professional organizations such as bar associations—to provide the MİT with any requested data, documents, or information regarding certain crimes, such as crimes against the security of the state, national security, state secrets, and espionage. Failure to comply can be punished with imprisonment. In a clause related to the MİT's ability to intercept and store private data on "external intelligence, national defense, terrorism, international crimes, and cyber-security passing through telecommunication channels," no requirement to procure a court order is mentioned.[111] The law also limits MİT agents' accountability for wrongdoing. Courts must obtain the permission of the head of the agency in order to investigate agents, and journalists or editors who publish leaks on MİT activities via media channels may be imprisoned for three to nine years. Some observers have argued that the bid to shield the MİT from judicial investigations was intended to provide legal cover for the agency's negotiations at the time with the PKK, which is officially ecognized as a terrorist organization; it also facilitated the crackdown on government opponents such as the Gülenists.[112]

The anonymous purchase of mobile phones is not allowed; buyers must provide official identification. According to a Council of Ministers decision dated 2000, Turkish citizens may only import one mobile phone every two years. Imported devices can be registered at mobile phone operators' subscription centers and an e-government website, for a fee of TRY 149.20 (US$40). Devices that are not registered within 60 days are shut off from telecommunications networks. In 2011, the BTK imposed regulations on the use of encryption hardware and software. Suppliers are required to provide encryption keys to state authorities before they can offer their products or services to individuals or companies within Turkey. Failure to comply can result in administrative fines and, in cases related to national security, prison sentences.

Under Law No. 5651, hosting and access providers must retain all traffic info mation for one year and maintain the accuracy, integrity, and confidentiality f such data. In addition, access providers must file the data ogether with a time stamp and provide assistance and support to the TİB (now the BTK) in monitoring internet traffic On December 8, 2015, the Constitutional Cou t nullified a set of amendments passed in February 2014, including a requirement that hosting providers must store data for up to two years.[113] The decision entered into force in December 2016.

Public-use internet providers hold different responsibilities depending on their status as either

---

110   For a history of interception of communications, see Faruk Bildirici, *Gizli Kulaklar Ulkesi* [The Country of Hidden Ears] (Istanbul: Iletisim, 1999); Enis Coskun, *Kuresel Gozatti: Elektronik Gizli Dinleme ve Goruntuleme* [Global Custody: Electronic Interception of Communications and Surveillance] (Ankara: Umit Yayincilik, 2000).
111   Human Rights Watch, "Turkey: Internet Freedom, Rights in Sharp Decline," September 2, 2014, http://bit.ly/1r1kJ0F
112   See Sebnem Arsu, "Turkish Leader Signs Bill Expanding Spy Agency's Power," *New York Times*, dated April 25, 2014, http://nyti.ms/1McuXsn
; and Fehim Taştekin, "Is Turkey reverting to a 'muhaberat' state?" *Al-Monitor*, April 17, 2014, http://bit.ly/1NDF1h7
113   Burçak Unsal, "The Constitutional Court's decision on internet law," *Hurriyet Daily News*, December 14, 2015 http://www.hurriyetdailynews.com/the-constitutional-courts-decision-on-internet-law.aspx?pageID=238&nID=92470&NewsCatID=396

TURKEY

commercial or noncommercial. Commercial providers are defined as entities that p ovide internet service for a certain payment, such as internet cafés. Noncommercial public-use internet providers are defined as entities that p ovide internet service at a certain venue for a certain period of time, such as in hotels and restaurants. While all public-use internet providers are expected to take measures to prevent access to criminal content and store internal IP distribution logs, commercial providers must also receive permission from the local administration, use a content-fil ering service approved by the BTK, and keep accurate daily records of internal IP distribution logs using software supplied by the BTK, which must be stored for a period of one year. In addition, these commercial providers are required to install a video surveillance system so as to identify users, and retain such records for seven days. All data must be made available to the BTK upon request—and without the need for a court order—under penalty of TRY 10,000 to 100,000 (US$2,600 to US$26,000) in fines [114]

In a largely positive development, a new Data Protection Law entered into force on April 7, 2016, aligning the country's legislation with European Union standards.[115]

Intimidation and Violence

Since January 2016, the International Press Institute (IPI) has collected at least 760 instances of abusive behavior against journalists online and 176 threats of violence.[116] A Twitter account (@ustakiloyunlari) "with over 100,000 followers has regularly smeared journalists and threatened to release personal information about them. Speech on Islam or the prophet Muhammad, posts about the "Kurdish problem," and even mild criticism of the president, government, or ruling party can result in death threats and legal battles. Citizen journalists and reporters for online news outlets operate in an environment in which media workers have often been physically assaulted for their reporting, and in some cases, killed.[117]

Technical Attacks

News sites have frequently come under technical attack at politically sensitive moments or after publishing controversial information. The arts-and-culture news website Sanatatak.com suffered technical attacks after publishing a letter supporting Turkish actress Füsun Demirel, who declared that she "wanted to be to be a [Kurdish] guerrilla" in her youth. The website was inaccessible for about 48 hours in March 2016 due to distributed denial-of-service (DDoS) attacks.[118] The HDP's website was attacked two days before the June 2015 elections and could not be accessed for over 24 hours. Popular news organizations such as *Zaman*, *Today's Zaman*, Cihan News Agency, *Rotahaber*,

114   For further information on this section, see Representative on Freedom of the Media, "Briefing on P oposed Amendments to Law No. 5651," Organization for Security and Co-operation in Europe, January 2014, http://www.osce.org/fom/110823?download=true; Center for Internet and Society, Stanford Law School, "WILMAP: Turkey," accessed November 6, 2014, http://stanford.io/1YcN8EX

115   Naz Degirmenci, "Turkey's First Comprehensive Data Protection Law Comes Into Force," Inside Privacy, April 8, 2016, https://www.insideprivacy.com/data-security/turkeys-fi st-comprehensive-data-protection-law-comes-into-force/

116   The OnTheLine Database Tracking Online Harassment of Journalists, http://onthelinedb.ipi.media

117   "25 journalists killed in Turkey," Reporters Without Borders, accessed October 2017, https://cpj.org/killed/europe/turkey/, and "Hurriyet columnist Ahmet Hakan injured in 'organized assault'," *Hurriyet Daily News*, October 1, 2015, http://www.hurriyetdailynews.com/hurriyet-columnist-ahmet-hakan-injured-in-organized-assault.aspx?pageID=238&nID=89212&NewsCatID=509

118   "In Turkey, technical attacks imperil digital media survival," International Press Institute, April 12, 2016, http://www.freemedia.at/in-turkey-technical-attacks-compromise-digital-media-sustainability/

TURKEY

Radikal, Sözcü, and *Taraf* reported cyberattacks against their websites during the November 2015 elections.

While opposition news sites and Twitter accounts are frequently targeted by progovernment hackers, government ministers have also been affected. RedHack's penetration of the personal email account of Berat Albayrak yielded more than 57,000 messages from 2000 to 2016, including many that covered state affairs. The material was uploaded to Dropbox, OneDrive, GitHub, and Google Drive in October 2016. In January 2017, the BTK announced that the government would set up an army of "white-hat hackers" to defend Turkey in cyberspace.[119]

---

119   Baris Simsek, "'White hat' hackers team to defend Turkey," Daily Sabah, January 14, 2017, https://www.dailysabah.com/turkey/2017/01/14/white-hat-hackers-team-to-defend-turkey

---

This is an official publication of the
**Commission on Security and
Cooperation in Europe.**

This publication is intended to document
developments and trends in participating
States of the Organization for Security
and Cooperation in Europe (OSCE).

All Commission publications may be freely
reproduced, in any form, with appropriate
credit. The Commission encourages
the widest possible dissemination
of its publications.

http://www.csce.gov   @HelsinkiComm

The Commission's Web site provides
access to the latest press releases
and reports, as well as hearings and
briefings. Using the Commission's electronic
subscription service, readers are able
to receive press releases, articles,
and other materials by topic or countries
of particular interest.

Please subscribe today.